CONTENTS

4   CONTENTS

4

COME AWAY

How to Have a Personal Prayer Retreat

SHEL ARENSEN

Kregel
Publications

For my lovely wife, Kym, who
has struggled together with me in
prayer. May all the glory go to
God, the Almighty One.

Come Away: How to Have a Personal Prayer Retreat

© 2003 by Shel Arensen

Published by Kregel Publications, a division of Kregel, Inc.,
P.O. Box 2607, Grand Rapids, MI 49501.

Unless otherwise indicated, Scripture quotations are from the
Holy Bible, New International Version®. © 1973, 1978, 1984
by International Bible Society. Used by permission of
Zondervan Publishing House. All rights reserved.

Scripture quotations marked KJV are from the King James
version of the Holy Bible.

Library of Congress Cataloging-in-Publication Data
Come away: how to have a personal prayer retreat / by
Shel Arensen
     p. cm.
     1. Spiritual Retreats—Christianity. 2. Prayer—
Christianity. I. Title.
BV5068.R4 A74   2003
248.3'2—dc21   2002152253

ISBN 0-8254-2043-1

Printed in the United States of America

03 04 05 06 07 / 5 4 3 2 1

FOREWORD

"MY SHEEP LISTEN TO MY VOICE," Jesus said. Have you been listening to his voice lately? Have you been putting your ear to his Word and asking him to speak to you?

Have you been sitting at the feet of Jesus, as Mary of Bethany did, turning your back on a thousand distractions to enjoy the presence of your bridegroom, the carpenter from Nazareth—the one who said he was going to prepare a place for you and coming back to get you so you can be with him forever?

We were made for a person and a place. Jesus is the person. Heaven is the place. We'll never be satisfied with any person less than Jesus, and no place less than heaven. We won't be fully content until we're home with our Beloved. But the closest we can get to contentment—and to heaven—while we're still here as aliens and strangers on this earth, is when we come away with Jesus and get away from his substitutes.

Shel Arensen is right on target when he says, "Whether we realize it or not, we desperately need to spend time with God." Many of us realize it, but only sporadically. No sooner do we sense he's the one we're longing for, that he's the cold refreshment for our parched

5

throats, than we turn to lesser streams that cannot quench our thirst. We let that still small voice of God get buried under the din of our busyness. Television, radio, e-mail, classes, sports, business trips, chores, hobbies. Up early, to bed late. Music turned up loud. Talk shows where we hear from everybody but the One who knows everything.

How does this all fit with "Be still, and know that I am God?"

John Piper says God is most glorified in us when we are most satisfied in him. We will only be satisfied with God if we go out of our way to spend special time with him.

In the spring of 1988, Nanci and I and our daughters, Karina and Angela, then only seven and nine, spent two weeks with Shel and Kym Arensen and their children in their home in Kenya. We'll never forget those people or that place. We celebrated Easter in a large hut with backless benches, worshiping God for hours, delighting to the children as they danced to the music. We looked down over the Great Rift Valley and listened to the monkeys chatter in the trees over our heads.

Sitting here in my office in Oregon, I just turned my head to the left to see a picture I took there of a tall young Maasai woman and her child, who seemed to appear out of nowhere as we picnicked on a game reserve with the Arensens. We still have a Maasai spear in our basement.

We saw wildebeests and zebras, giraffes and gazelles, heard lions and saw hippo tracks outside our tent. Baboons chased our four-wheeler. (We found out later the Arensen boys were throwing cheese snacks out the sunroof.) We drove to the coast, to Malindi, where Shel warned us to run through the shallow waters into the Indian Ocean to avoid burning our feet. (In Oregon you run through ocean water for another reason—to keep your feet from getting numb!)

We saw insects so big they cast shadows. Early one morning our daughters looked at us wide-eyed and one of them said, "Daddy, there's a giant leaf with legs standing over my hairbrush." I went into the bathroom and stopped in my tracks. It was . . . well, a giant leaf with legs, straddling a hairbrush. I've never seen an insect like it before or since.

Kenya is an exotic place, but what we saw that really stuck with us was more than these things I've recounted. It was the quality of Kym and Shel's life. We saw the fruit of Shel's years as editor (following in his father's footsteps) of *Today in Africa*, a quality Christian magazine that built up the body of Christ and reached out to unbelievers. We saw how the Arensens cared for people and built their family around the things that matter.

Years later Nanci and I sat with Shel and Kym in Oregon, where they told us that they believed God was calling them to step away from the work they'd been doing all those years. Not content to be comfortable, they wanted to start a new missions adventure, to evangelize and plant churches among the unreached Dorobo people, a tribe of hunters and gatherers.

Fantastic, we said. Wow, we said. To step from a long-term established ministry in Kenya to such a work among an unreached tribe was as radical as it would have been for us to leave America for Africa.

But they did it, crying out to God to prepare the way for them. God answered that prayer powerfully. And now there are over five hundred Dorobo people who know Jesus Christ as their Savior, and more than twenty churches planted among the Dorobo where there were none before.

I tell this story for one simple reason—if I'm reading a book on prayer, I want to know whether the person writing it has walked with God in the crucible of life, drawing on his strength to do what could not be done without him. Shel and Kym Arensen have. So what's on these pages is more than just words.

This isn't only a good book on prayer retreats; it's a good book on prayer. It's full of Scripture, which has a power nothing else does. (God never says our points and anecdotes won't return unto him without accomplishing their purpose—he says his Word won't.) It's simple yet profound. It's clearly written, as you might expect from someone whose job for many years has been putting truth into understandable terms. It's richly illustrated, with a fascinating African flavor, but readily cross-cultural. It's practical. You won't just walk away with theory, but specific ideas of what you can do to come away with God and enjoy his presence.

What could be more important—and more satisfying—than to set aside time to confess, give thanks to the Lord, recognize his greatness, intercede for others, open his Word and seek after God?

I enjoy regular time with God and have had prayer and Bible study retreats before. Some of my sweetest memories are of days given over to God—having meals with just him, taking a long bike ride with him, talking with him, reading good books with him by my side, listening to his Word and asking him to speak to me. But as I read this excellent book, I realized it's been too long since I carved one of these times into my schedule. Well, I fixed that. I picked some spots on my calendar and wrote in God's name. After reading this book, I think you'll likely do the same. I'm looking forward to those days. So will you.

"Open your servant's eyes," Elisha prayed. And God did open his eyes, to the invisible realities of the spirit realm we're often blind to. May our eyes be opened as we step into the unseen realm to walk with God, and he steps into this realm to walk with us. May he use *Come Away* to draw us into his presence and empower us in a way that changes the world around us.

—R<small>ANDY</small> A<small>LCORN</small>

ACKNOWLEDGMENTS

I WOULD LIKE TO THANK Dr. Jay Rupp and Rev. Jack Taylor, mentors and examples to me in prayer. Thanks also to Mary MacCallum, David and Theresa Knauss, Pat Thurman, Joseph Kim, John and Sandy Nelson, the Taylor family, Len and Vera Russell, Rev. Dave Zetterberg, Pastor Samuel Ng'ang'a, Sarababi and the other Dorobo believers, and my own children, Heath, Reid, Blake, and Malindi, for allowing me to use their stories about prayer.

INTRODUCTION

A YOUNG MAN BUTTONHOLED me and demanded, "How did you do that?" Thinking he'd been impressed by my missions talk, I began to give points on friendship evangelism and church planting.

"No, no! Not that!" the man said, slightly annoyed. "I want to know how you spent a whole day praying. How do you do that?"

I had shared with the church class our work in Kenya among a group of hunter-gatherers known as the Dorobo. I mentioned that my wife and I had spent a day in prayer before venturing into a new area of the forest and how God had used that prayer time to start a new church.

This young man wanted to know how anyone could pray for a day. Praying for ten minutes was hard enough.

I didn't have a quick answer. I said something about scheduling time, going someplace alone, bringing our needs to God, reading the Bible, and singing praise songs. But I really didn't know how to tell someone to pray for a day.

I was just learning myself.

I've never considered myself very good at praying. About ten years ago I asked God to make me a man of prayer. I can't say my

11

prayer has been fully answered, but I'm learning and growing in the area of prayer. One big step in my spiritual journey has been setting aside time for personal prayer retreats.

When I first thought about praying for a whole day, I felt dismay. Like the young man after that class, I wondered, "How could I ever do that? What would I say to God for that long?"

I had taken part in our yearly mission prayer days, at which we received reams of requests and gathered in small groups to pray. Even speed-readers could hardly pray for all the requests on those lists. When we had finished, I felt relieved. Duty done, I wouldn't have to face that again until next year's day of prayer.

But as God began working in my life to make me more of a man of prayer, I learned the importance of taking an extended time to talk with God. A personal prayer retreat provides time to get re-acquainted with God, a time to awaken our first love for the Savior, a time to groan and bring our deepest problems to the Problem-Solver, and a time to seek God's face and ask for his guidance.

Squeezed for Time

Finding time to pray has always been difficult for me. It seems I always have other, more important things to do. I know nothing should be more important than prayer, but pressing matters crowd in and strangle my time alone with the Lord.

As a missionary in Kenya, surely I should be a shining example of a prayer warrior. Don't get me wrong. I do pray, but it's a struggle finding the time to spend alone with the Lord. Needs are great. When a man and his wife showed up at 6 A.M., carrying a baby who was dying of pneumonia, could I tell them to wait while I had my prayer time? We prayed as the frail child labored for every breath in the car as we drove to medical care. So much for time alone with the Lord that day.

Not every day brings a life-or-death interruption, but every day brings its own steady flow of needs and must-do items. Our swollen schedules include commuting and work, family and fun. We make room for sports, hobbies, and TV. As Christians we attend church and have fellowship with other believers. Where are hours to spend with God in prayer when it's hard enough to carve out ten or fifteen minutes from our day to pray and read the Word? In a world of one-minute Bibles and instant messages, why would anyone be talking about daylong prayer retreats?

Because whether we realize it or not, we desperately need to spend time with God.

Desperation Leads to Day of Prayer

That prayer day I mentioned at the beginning of the introduction didn't happen because I had well meaning plans to know God better and improve my spiritual life. I spent that day in prayer out of desperation. God put me in a situation where I could not rely on my own strength or ability, and I needed God.

My wife, Kym, and I had worked for about twelve years in Kenya in a Christian literature ministry, publishing a youth magazine and training Kenyan writers and editors. As we turned this work over to capable Kenyans, the Lord called us to the unreached Dorobo tribe, a small group of hunters and honey-collectors in the highland forests who desperately needed to hear the gospel. As we started evangelism and church planting among the Dorobo, I realized I didn't know what to do. I offered up a simple prayer to God. Help!

As a trained journalist, I knew how to interview, write, edit, and publish a magazine, and I could teach others to do the same. But going into a village where I knew no one? Where I didn't understand the culture? Where language would be a barrier? Where should I start?

We started with God because he'd called us into this new venture. We knew God was trustworthy and we had nowhere else to turn. Our prayer life became an attitude of dependence upon God. As we prayed, the Lord gave my wife a promise from Zechariah 4:6: "'Not by might nor by power, but by my Spirit,' says the LORD Almighty." God's Spirit would do the work of bringing the Dorobo to faith in Christ.

We prayed about every new step. We put maps of the area on the floor of our living room and prayed over them. A prayer band of missionary teachers from Rift Valley Academy, a school for missionary children in Kenya, had committed themselves to praying until God brought the gospel to the Dorobo. We recruited others from our home churches in the U.S. to pray. We covered this new ministry in prayer.

We decided to spend two days doing evangelism in the Keringet Forest. My wife and I prayed and asked God to show us how to reach this group with the gospel. But even then we didn't set aside a special day of prayer for our outreach to the Dorobo.

We had scheduled the trip for the dry season in the middle of January. But a huge thunderstorm washed out the road to Keringet. I felt confused. Hadn't we prayed? We didn't know if God hadn't heard our prayers or if we'd awakened Satan, and he'd blocked our way. We felt discouraged. How could we bring the gospel if we couldn't even get into the village? With our trip canceled, my wife suggested we set aside the next day for prayer. Since I'd already scheduled that day to be with the Dorobo, I agreed.

After sending our kids off to school, Kym and I took our Bibles and hiked to a quiet spot in the forest near our home. We praised the Lord and gave thanks for prayers God had already answered. We read Scripture to remind ourselves of God's power. We prayed and pleaded with God to prepare the hearts of the people in the Keringet area to receive the gospel. We prayed for wisdom as we planned another trip to Keringet.

At about 2 P.M., we stopped so we could be home when the boys arrived from school. We felt encouraged by the Word that God still reigned as king of the universe, and he had control of this world. The Lord did not give us a specific plan and date to go to Keringet, but we felt confident that God, by the work of his Spirit, would go before us and reach the Dorobo.

We prayed that day because we had to. We needed God and his direction. That prayer retreat didn't feel like a burden. It wasn't a duty. Instead, we had a special time with God. We got close to God our Father and asked him what to do.

God Responds to the Prayer Retreat

Two weeks after our prayer day, we received a letter from Silas, a Kenyan pastor who felt God calling him to Keringet. I met with him, and we helped him set up a few months later. Within a year, Silas had a church of about twenty and had already baptized six of them.

God had answered our prayers offered during our miniretreat in the forest. He hadn't used us in the way we thought he would. Instead, he brought Silas to us. During our day of prayer, we got to know God better. Our faith had grown as we had a chance to see God at work, and a church sprouted in the Keringet forest. God honored the time we dedicated to seeking his face.

I Need You, God

We need God. We may think we're doing okay. We may cover up our needs and problems and keep up a surface-level Christianity. But deep down in our hearts, we all desperately need more of God in our lives. Unless we gain an awareness of our need, we will not desire to spend more time with him in prayer.

Often God allows us to go through hard times to bring us to the end of our strength. At these times of desperation, we are finally ready to throw ourselves before him. One purpose of this book is to create the awareness that we need more of God, which stimulates a hunger to know God more intimately. The other purpose is to help plan personal retreats—as long as a day or a weekend—in prayer.

Jesus often withdrew to be alone with the Father. This book is intended to encourage you to follow the example of our Lord Jesus and learn to desire and enjoy time alone with God.

PART ONE

THREE REASONS FOR EXTENDED TIMES OF PRAYER

THE FOLLOWING PAGES SHOW how to plan and practice personal prayer in retreats, but why should we invest that much time in prayer? Why should you have a time of prayer that lasts for several hours or even a whole day? Three main reasons can be given for setting aside a retreat time for prayer.

The first reason, which will be covered in chapter 1, is to seek God's face and know him better. The church is the bride of Christ (Eph. 5:23–32; Rev. 19:7; 21:9). If we are in a marriage relationship with the God of the universe, how well do we know our husband? As in any marriage, the only way to get to know our spouse is to take time to be alone together and to talk and learn to understand each other. Likewise, if we want a closer relationship with God, we need to invest time.

The second reason for a prayer retreat, as shall be seen in chapter 2, is to ask for understanding, guidance, and wisdom. God has promised to give us wisdom when we ask (James 1:5). He wants to show us the way. The Spirit of God dwells in our hearts and we have the very mind of Christ. So why are we so often lost? Hearing God's voice and understanding his will takes time.

The third chapter focuses on bringing prayer burdens to the Lord. Jesus told us to come to him if we are weary and carrying a heavy burden (Matt. 11:28–30). We often carry the burdens of concern and worry when God wants us to meet with him and leave the problems at his feet.

These are three distinct reasons for spending time alone with God. But they blur, so that any prayer retreat probably has elements of all three.

one

SEEKING GOD'S FACE

Glory in his holy name; let the hearts of those who seek the
LORD rejoice. Look to the LORD and his strength; seek his
face always.

—1 Chronicles 16:10–11

THE FIRST GOAL, WHEN SETTING aside a time for a prayer retreat, should
be to seek God's face. We want to know him better. As we realize
anew who our God is, it refocuses our lives.

Our God is the sovereign King of this universe.

Our God loves us enough to die for us.

Our God is holy and dwells in unapproachable light. Yet, despite
our sin, he ripped open the curtain that separated us from God's
holy presence. This happened when Jesus himself, through his
death, opened a way for us to come before God's throne of grace to
worship and bring our needs (Heb. 9:11–15).

As we learn to know God better, we will love him more and
crave time together with him. We'll understand him and know what
he wants in our lives. Our lifestyle will change, and we will see God
answer prayers as a result of our taking time to be alone with God.

But greater than all of these results is that God's name will be glorified and lifted up, especially as others see what he is doing in our lives. That's God's ultimate goal. God created us and called us into his kingdom for the praise of his glory (Eph. 1:11–12). As encountering God changes our lives, the Lord receives praise and glory.

Moses knew how important it was to take time to meet alone with God. He even pitched a special tent where they could be together. Here Moses boldly said to God, "Now show me your glory" (Exod. 33:18).

God Speaks with Moses Face to Face

The tent of overlapping animal skins stood some distance outside the camp of the Israelites (Exod. 33). Carrying his staff, the old man strode toward the tent. The men and women in the camp rose in reverence at the doors of their tents to watch as Moses entered his prayer tent—the tent of meeting. As Moses bent his head forward to walk into the tent, the pillar of cloud that shrouded God's glory descended and covered the entrance to the tent of meeting. Inside the tent, the Lord spoke to Moses face to face as a man speaks with his friend.

Moses sighed as he stood in God's presence, thinking how quickly the Israelites had abandoned God and worshiped a golden calf while he received the Ten Commandments on Mount Sinai. Moses had disciplined the people and then pleaded with the Lord to forgive them. Moses had even asked that his own name be blotted out of God's book if God refused to forgive the people.

The Lord replied, "Whoever has sinned against me I will blot out of my book. Now go, lead the people to the place I spoke of, and my angel will go before you. However, when the time comes for me to punish, I will punish them for their sin" (Exod. 32:33–

34). Then the Lord had sent a plague as a punishment on the Israelite camp because of their sin in worshiping the calf.

God repeated his command that Moses must lead the people up to the Promised Land. "But I will not go with you, because you are a stiff-necked people and I might destroy you on the way" (Exod. 33:3).

Moses had pondered this command. How could he lead this stubborn mob on his own? Now, in the tent of meeting, Moses poured out his heart.

"Lord," Moses said, "you have been telling me to lead these people. But they're so rebellious! I can't do this on my own. And now you're saying you won't go with us. Who will you send with me to lead them? You say you have known my name and you have found favor with me. If you're really pleased with me, then teach me your ways so I can continue to find favor with you in this job of leading the people. Remember, this nation is your people."

The Lord responded, "My Presence will go with you and I will give you rest."

"You must go with us," Moses said. "If your presence doesn't go with us, then don't send us up from this place. How will anyone know you're pleased with your people unless you go with us?"

The Lord answered, "I will do the very thing you have asked, because I'm pleased with you and I know you by name."

Satisfied that God's presence would stay with them, guiding them on the way, Moses made a bold request. "Now show me your glory."

> I will cause all my goodness to pass in front of you, and I will proclaim my name, the LORD, in your presence. I will have mercy on whom I will have mercy, and I will have compassion on whom I will have compassion. But . . . you cannot see my face, for no one may see me and live. . . . There is a place near me where you may stand on a rock. When my glory passes by, I will put you in a cleft in the

rock and cover you with my hand until I have passed by.
Then I will remove my hand and you will see my back; but
my face must not be seen. (Exod. 33:19–23)

God then instructed Moses to chisel out two new stone tablets
to write down God's commandments and to meet him on top of
Mount Sinai the next morning (Exod. 34). Moses obeyed and
climbed the mountain. The Lord came down in a cloud and stood
there with Moses and proclaimed his name. "I am *YHWH*, the LORD."
The Lord covered Moses in the cleft of the rock and then passed
before him, proclaiming, "The LORD, the LORD, the compassionate
and gracious God, slow to anger, abounding in love and faithfulness, maintaining love to thousands, and forgiving wickedness, rebellion and sin. Yet he does not leave the guilty unpunished; he
punishes the children and their children for the sin of the fathers to
the third and fourth generation" (vv. 6–7).

Moses, overwhelmed by seeing even the back of God's glory,
bowed to the ground and worshiped. "O Lord, if I have found favor
in your eyes, . . . then let the Lord go with us. Although this is a
stiff-necked people, forgive our wickedness and our sin, and take
us as your inheritance" (Exod. 34:9).

The Lord made a covenant with Moses and the nation of Israel,
and promised to show his power as they moved into the land of
promise. Then the Lord asked Moses to write down the words of
the covenant.

Moses stayed in God's presence forty days and forty nights without eating bread or drinking water, satisfied by God's presence and
speaking with the Holy One of Israel. When Moses came down off
the mountain, his face radiated because he had spoken with the
Lord. He had to put a veil over his face as he told Israel what God
wanted. But when Moses entered back into God's presence in the
tent of meeting, he would remove the veil and speak with the Lord.

Moses spent time in God's presence and the Lord spoke with him as a man speaks with his friend.

David Writes: Seek God's Face Always

Time after time, David learned to turn to God in his troubles. David depended upon God and called out for help. David looked for God. He sought God's face. And David wanted to experience him more.

In a psalm David composed after he had brought the ark of the covenant to Jerusalem, David wrote, "Glory in his holy name; let the hearts of those who seek the LORD rejoice. Look to the LORD and his strength; seek his face always" (1 Chron. 16:10–11).

David had learned early to rely upon the Lord and his strength. He had seen God's faithfulness as he faced a lion and a bear that threatened to take his sheep (1 Sam. 17:32–37). God had been faithful as David stood against Goliath of Gath. David trusted as he learned to wait for God's timing, when he would be given the throne. During dark years of relentless pressure as he tried to stay a step ahead of Saul and the armies of Israel (e.g., 1 Sam. 26:13–25), David learned to seek God's face and rejoice in the Lord (e.g., Ps. 63).

And as David thought back over all God had done, he composed the song recorded in 1 Chronicles 16 and gave it to Asaph, his chief choir director. David wanted the people of Israel always to seek God's face.

The white-haired man limped slightly as he moved slowly across the flat paving stones of the palace. He could feel every ache and creak in his bones, reminding him of old battle injuries and hard nights spent sleeping in caves. He smiled at the young man who stood, leaning on his outstretched arms against the waist-high porch wall. King David gripped his son's shoulder and the two looked over the growing city of Jerusalem. David pointed out the site he'd selected for the temple that Solomon would build. "This is your kingdom," David stated. "Rule it well."

"Oh father," Solomon pleaded, "I don't know where to start."

David's eyes gazed far beyond the city walls to the mountains of Judah where he once guarded his father's sheep. In his mind he saw the lion and the bear. He remembered the giant. He recalled the frantic days of living as a fugitive in caves. He remembered how he had learned to trust in God.

David spoke softly, "Nothing is more important than this, my son. Devote your heart and soul to seeking the Lord your God. Listen, Solomon my son, and acknowledge the God of your father, and serve him with wholehearted devotion and with a willing mind, for the Lord searches every heart and understands every motive behind the thoughts. If you seek him, he will be found by you; but if you forsake him, he will reject you forever" (see 1 Chron. 28:9).

Solomon followed his father's advice. As he assumed the throne of Israel, Solomon went to the tent at Gibeon that contained the ark of the covenant. Solomon brought a large group of leaders with him, and then offered a thousand burnt offerings on the bronze altar and inquired of the Lord (1 Kings 3:4).

The word translated "to inquire" is the same David used in his psalm to "seek" the Lord always, and when he advised Solomon to "seek" the Lord and to devote his heart and soul to "seeking" the Lord. Solomon began by inquiring of the Lord or seeking God's face. That night, God answered Solomon, appearing in a vision and offering to give Solomon whatever he asked for. Solomon asked for wisdom, which he received along with wealth and honor (vv. 5–15).

If You Seek Me, You Will Find Me

God wants us to seek his face. God wants us to find him. David told Solomon that if he sought the Lord, Solomon would find the Lord. This advice is based on a promise God gave to Israel in the Law. God had warned Moses that if Israel didn't follow the commands and demands of the law, he would scatter them among the nations. Then the Lord gave this promise in Deuteronomy 4:29: "But if from there you seek the LORD your God, you will find him if you look for him with all your heart and with all your soul."

God wants his people to seek him. Even if they've gone astray and fallen into all kinds of sin, God's voice still calls: "If you seek me, you will find me." David looked for God with all his heart and soul and he found God. Then David took this promise and passed it on to Solomon. If we seek God, he will be found. It's not because of what we do, but because God is willing to be found by those who take the time to seek his face.

Jeremiah, writing at a time when Judah stood at the verge of being scattered to the nations for their sinfulness, saw the same promise in Deuteronomy while studying the scroll of the Law, and he repeated it for the people. "Then you will call upon me and come and pray to me, and I will listen to you. You will seek me and find me when you seek me with all your heart. I will be found by you" (Jer. 29:12–14a). Even as we seek, God allows himself to be found. God wants men to seek him because he wants to be found. God shows himself to those who seek him.

As we think about taking time for a prayer retreat, we need to keep this truth in mind. We are seeking God's face. We want our experience with God to change how we live. And we want our Lord to be glorified. That glory will be seen not because we are great, nor because we're spiritual giants who've taken extra time to pray. Rather, because people will see the Father reflected in us, especially as we take time to know our God and seek his face. As we know God better, our lives will change.

Now Is the Time to Seek the Lord

Hosea tells us that now is the time to seek the Lord: "Sow for yourselves righteousness, reap the fruit of unfailing love, and break up your unplowed ground; for it is time to seek the LORD, until he comes and showers righteousness on you" (Hos. 10:12).

A big part of seeking God means breaking up the unplowed ground. The unplowed ground is our hard, self-reliant hearts. As we come before God in prayer, he will show us his holiness and make us aware of our sins. Then, as we repent and bow before God with humble hearts, he can forgive us, cleanse us, and cover us with the righteousness of our Lord Jesus.

Mary MacCallum never considered having a personal prayer retreat until a few years ago. Then she attended a meeting where a speaker encouraged both private and communal retreats. Mary felt drawn to the idea, but it took her a few years to schedule the retreat into her busy life. She rented a cottage on a lake for six days. She looked forward to a time of worship, cleansing, and healing in her body, soul, and spirit.

To facilitate the cleansing and healing of her body, Mary held a special fast, eating only fruit and not drinking any caffeine during those six days. Mary also decided to walk to promote physical cleansing and healing. She set a goal of walking up to eight hours each day. She didn't reach her goal, but she did walk seven hours on the last day. Mary regarded her dieting, walking, and other exercises as acts of worship.

Before the retreat, Mary had been memorizing the book of Ephesians and had finished chapter 3 and part of chapter 4. During her prayer retreat, she chose to meditate on the verses she had memorized whenever she walked or laid down. Meditating on those verses helped Mary listen to Lord. As she repeated the verses in her mind, she found herself speaking to God and discussing what he had written in his Word. Mary also worshiped God through this time of meditation.

When not walking or lying down, Mary exercised her mind by memorizing more verses in Ephesians. This was another act of worship.

As Mary spent her prayer retreat in Ephesians, she felt impressed by God's incomparably great power—a power strong enough to raise Christ from the dead. As she walked and talked to God about his Word, Mary began to covet the power described in Ephesians 3:18 to grasp the fullness of the love of Christ and the power to know this unknowable love. As Mary prayed, she asked God to help her to know that love as it was poured out on her by God. And she pleaded to be able to grasp and know that love for others so she could pour love out to others as she received it from God.

Mary's prayer retreat stands as a powerful week in her life and she plans to experience more like it.

As the Deer Pants for Water

I learned to set aside days for prayer when I desperately needed God's help. The sons of Korah use a similar word picture to describe a heart that longs to know God. "As the deer pants for streams of water, so my soul pants for you, O God. My soul thirsts for God, for the living God. When can I go and meet with God?" (Ps. 42:1–2).

I once watched animals at a waterhole in Kenya. The zebras edged up skittishly, their stripes blending them into the dry scrub brush that surrounded the pond. They stared at the water. We could see they wanted a drink. But to reach the water, they had to leave the protection of the bush and cross twenty-five meters of red, cracked mud that ringed the pool.

The zebras knew this made them vulnerable to attack by lions that often set up shop around the waterhole. The zebras stood back, velvet-black noses twitching as they smelled what they needed so much—water. Finally, when they could hold back no longer, the zebras cantered up to the water, drank deeply, and then dashed back into the covering thickets.

Those zebras needed water so badly that nothing could hold them back. God wants us to desire him in the same way. God wants us to pant after him. When we have that desperate need for God, we're ready to seek God's face and set aside a day to pray.

two

ASKING FOR UNDERSTANDING AND GUIDANCE

You guide me with your counsel, and afterward you will take me into glory.

—Psalm 73:24

ONE REASON TO HAVE A PRAYER retreat is to ask God for guidance and understanding on a big decision. We all want to know God's will before stepping out. We want to be sure we're doing the right thing. But how do we find God's will?

We see priests in the Old Testament throwing the *urim* and then discerning God's will from the way they fell on the ground. We see the eleven disciples casting lots to choose a replacement for Judas Iscariot (Acts 1:15–26). Can't we do the same?

We see Rebekah puzzled at the unborn twins twisting and punching within her. She prays and asks God what's going on, and he speaks to her and tells her two nations are already fighting in her womb (Gen. 25:21–26). The Israelites sought God's will about disputes and problems facing them. They came to elders appointed to assist Moses, who mediated and inquired of the Lord's will (Exod. 18:13–27).

Where Are the Donkeys?

It would be nice to have a seer cast lots and tell us what God's will is. It would be easy to call in a prophet and ask him to reveal God's will for us. That's what Saul did (1 Sam. 9).

Before Saul became the first King of Israel, his father Kish woke him up one morning. "Saul, hurry! The donkeys broke free from their tether last night. They're gone. Quick, take one of the servants and go find the donkeys. I'm afraid some dishonest person will find them and sell them or keep them as his own."

Saul and the servant followed the tracks, but on the main path, the donkeys' hoof prints joined hundreds of other footprints of people and animals, and they lost the trail. Saul passed through the hill country of Ephraim, and finding no trace of the lost donkeys, he gave up. He turned to his servant and said, "Let's go home. By now my father Kish will be more worried about us than the donkeys."

But Saul's servant said, "There's a man of God in this town. He is highly respected and everything he says comes true. He's a true prophet of God. Why don't we go ask him where the donkeys are? Maybe he'll show us which road to take."

Saul and his servant found the man of God, Samuel, who told Saul the donkeys had already been found. Then Samuel anointed Saul as the first king of Israel, and the Spirit of God came on him as he began to lead the kingdom of Israel.

God showed Saul where his donkeys had gone. God does give guidance, even in mundane decisions and questions. But it doesn't seem to happen very often anymore.

Many African Christians struggle with this dilemma. Under African traditional religion, they went to a seer or a healer who would ask for a sacrifice and then inquire of the spirits. Africans were used to a system where they could learn the exact cause of a certain problem or disease and what needed to be done to get rid of it. The guidance might not always have been correct, but it was clear, and the people always knew what course of action to take.

Many Africans have struggled with Christianity because, as a system, it doesn't give that kind of clear guidance. So when they can't get the clear guidance they're looking for, they are often tempted to go back to the traditional diviner to find out what to do.

God's Revealed Will

We do have the revealed will of God in the Bible. We can study the Bible and know that when it says in 1 Thessalonians 4:3, "It is God's will that you should be sanctified: that you should avoid sexual immorality," then we should not be involved in sexual immorality or we'll be outside of God's revealed will. That kind of guidance is clear from God's Word.

But what about such questions as "Where should I go to college?" "Should I take a job in another state?" "Should we adopt an AIDS orphan?" None of the possible responses stands clearly outside God's will as it is revealed in the Bible. So how do we decide? Paul tells us in 1 Corinthians 2:14–16 that we have the Spirit of God within us, and that we have the mind of Christ. So how can we know what the Lord wants us to do on a certain matter?

I think we should start with prayer. We need to seek God's face and make our lives right before God. Then we should ask God to show us his mind on the matter. We must know God's Word well enough that we don't make a decision that would violate God's revealed will in the Bible. God also uses counselors and advisers. We should not neglect asking other believers for advice. God can also lead by circumstances, opening and closing doors to show us what to do. We also need to take into account our own feelings and desires and those of our family members when we make certain decisions. And the Lord has given each of us common sense. All these ingredients need to be thrown into the pot for a good decision-making stew.

But in addition, we must put in a heavy dose of prayer. Praying for understanding takes time. We can't expect to pray for a few minutes and then have God give us a flash of inspiration. We are usually so caught up in our own will and desire that it takes time to know God's will and his heart on a matter. That's why it's important to set aside time to pray and ask the Lord for guidance.

Asking for Guidance About Adoption

The first time my wife and I set aside a day for prayer, we wanted to adopt a baby girl to join the three sons in our family. My wife had been adopted, and she wanted to pass that gift on to a child who needed a home.

In 1984, we had prayed and made inquiries with agencies and Oregon Children's Services. We didn't have the money needed for private adoption, and the state of Oregon bluntly stated that if we already had children of our own, we'd never be considered as adoptive parents for kids in their system. We continued to pray and ask God to open a door, if this was his plan.

Four years later we were back in the United States for a one-year home assignment. Again we made inquiries. Suddenly we heard from a private agency about a baby soon to be born in Colorado. The mother wanted the child adopted into a Christian family, specifically a missionary family. We were excited and contacted the private adoption agency. But then the mother began asking for money to help her pay rent and other needs. Moreover, she wouldn't sign any papers relinquishing rights to her baby. We could pay a lot of money and still not be allowed to adopt this baby. We didn't know what to do. Should we pay the mother's rent? Should we pursue adoption at all? We just didn't know which way to proceed.

We decided to set aside a day to pray and ask for God's guidance. We knew from many Bible stories that God did give guidance to those who prayed and asked. And we knew that many Christians had taken a day to pray and seek God's guidance. We had often prayed and asked for God's guidance, but we had never taken a full day to do it.

We sent our boys off to school and drove to Oxbow Park on the Sandy River. There, we found a quiet spot near the river and prayed. We had brought our Bibles along, and we read from Psalms and praised God. We confirmed that our desire to adopt was within God's revealed will by reading James 1:27, which says, "Religion that God our Father accepts as pure and faultless is this: to look after orphans and widows in their distress and to keep oneself from being polluted by the world." But mostly we prayed and asked God to show us what to do.

By the end of the day, we felt we knew God's heart. He did want us to care for the orphans, and he did want us to open our home to a child or children in need of care. But we also felt that this child in Colorado wasn't the child God wanted us to adopt. So we went home, called the adoption agency to say we would not be able to proceed with the adoption of that baby. And we began to pray and ask God to show us the child or children he did want us to adopt.

Soon after that, Oregon Children's Services told us they had changed their policy of only placing children in homes where the couple had no children. Now they looked for homes with experienced parents to take care of their children. They interviewed us, did a home study, and we waited.

For a time it seemed we might be given three siblings. We were one of two families considered at the caseworkers' last meeting. But they decided to give those children to another family. We had no time to be disappointed, though, because one of the social workers at that meeting contacted us and said that when she looked at the information about our family, she knew we would provide the perfect home for a newborn baby she needed to place. After a whirlwind two weeks, we drove to a foster home to collect our new baby daughter, Malindi.

At the beginning we had been told Oregon Children's Services never had babies for adoption, and they never placed children in homes that already had children. But God gave us a baby. And it started with a day of prayer in Oxbow Park, seeking God's guidance.

One of the first things we need before we can come to God and ask his leading or guidance on an issue is to have our hearts right and humble before God. We can't expect to hear God's voice and listen to his leading if we have sin in our lives.

Saul Fails to Find Guidance

King Saul illustrated this final failure to follow God (1 Sam. 28). Saul, his hair now peppered with gray and an uncontrollable twitch in his right cheek, stood at the edge of the tented camp at Gilboa. He looked down at the orderly row of Philistine tents at Shunnem and he felt an icy shiver in his gut. Abner, general of the Israelite army, crossed his arms and looked at the king. "Tell us how we should attack, sir," Abner said.

Saul, eyes blurred by tears, pushed past his general and hurried toward his tent. "We need to inquire of the Lord," he rasped. "I'm going to sleep. Maybe the Lord will speak to me by a dream." Saul pleaded with God for guidance, but in the morning he emerged from his tent gaunt-faced and in a foul temper. "I have not seen any visions in the night. Bring me a prophet. Or bring me a priest who can throw the urim so we can know God's leading on how to go into battle with the Philistines." But God did not answer Saul. In desperation, Saul sent his men to find a medium who could contact the realm of the dead. He disguised himself and went to find guidance from the witch at Endor.

More than anything, Saul wanted God's help and guidance. He inquired of the Lord, just as he did when he looked for his father's donkeys. But this time the Lord did not answer him. Why not? Saul wanted God's guidance, but he had not followed God's revealed guidelines in his life. He had pretty much ignored the Law that Moses had handed down to Israel, allowing his heart to be invaded by selfishness, pride, and jealousy. Saul had set up another god before the Holy One of Israel—that god was himself. Saul no longer sought God's face. He didn't make following God his first priority, just wanting God to show him what to do. So God did not answer him.

God is not a faucet we can turn on and off at our own convenience to find the answers we seek. No, we must first seek God's face. We must love the Lord our God will all our hearts, souls, and minds. And from that proper humble attitude before the Lord, we may inquire and he will guide us. But when he gives us guidance, we need to obey.

Shall We Go to War?

This is something King Jehoshaphat wasn't ready to do (1 Kings 22; 2 Chron. 18). King Jehoshaphat of Judah sat on his throne next to Israel's King Ahab at the threshing floor by the entrance to Samaria. "I've brought my soldiers and I'm ready to help you in this battle to regain the city of Ramoth Gilead from the king of Aram," Jehoshaphat said. "But before we set out, I'd like to inquire of the Lord. Let's ask a prophet for God's guidance before this battle."

"By all means," Ahab answered. "I have more than one." He clapped his hands and called for four hundred false prophets. They came and bowed before King Ahab. "Shall I go to war against Ramoth Gilead, or shall I refrain?" Ahab asked. "Go," the prophets answered. "The Lord will give Ramoth Gilead into your hands." Jehoshaphat felt a shiver of discomfort run down his back. He had devoted his life to following God and obeying God's commands. After wiping a thin sheen of sweat from his brow, Jehoshaphat leaned over to Ahab and asked, "Don't you have any prophets of the Lord who can pray to God for us."

Ahab scowled and then whined, "There's one prophet, but I don't like him. He never prophesies anything good about me."

"But he's a prophet of the Lord?" asked Jehoshaphat.

"Yes, he's a prophet of the Lord. But why do we need to listen to him? We have four hundred prophets here who have prophesied our victory. What does the voice of one more prophet matter? Let's go to war!"

"I want to hear the Lord's guidance before I go into battle," Jehoshaphat insisted.

Beckoning to one of his officials, Ahab commanded, "Go at once and get that crazy prophet Micaiah, son of Imlah!"

As the two kings waited for Micaiah, one of the prophets of Baal, Zedekiah, leapt in front of them waving some horns fashioned from iron. Flecks of spit sprayed Jehoshaphat's face as Zedekiah ranted, "You will gore the Arameans with these horns until they are destroyed."

"Attack and be victorious!" shouted the others. "The Lord will give Ramoth Gilead into your hand."

The official who summoned Micaiah told him to go along with the rest of the prophets and prophesy victory. But Micaiah, a man who had devoted his life to seeking the Lord, answered, "As surely as the Lord lives, I can tell the king only what the Lord tells me." And in his heart Micaiah cried out to God for guidance.

The official led Micaiah before the two kings. Ahab glared down at the man of God, who was dressed in a simple robe. "Micaiah," the king asked, "shall we go to war against Ramoth Gilead, or shall I refrain?"

"Attack and be victorious," Micaiah mocked, copying the tone of voice of the other prophets, "for the Lord will give them into the king's hand."

"I can see you're making fun of my prophets again. How many times do I have to make you swear to tell me nothing but the truth?"

Micaiah shut his eyes and prayed. The two kings waited expectantly. Even the prophets dropped their hubbub to a murmur. Then Micaiah answered, "I saw Israel scattered on the hills like sheep without a shepherd. The Lord said these people no longer have a master. Let them go home in peace."

Ahab turned to Jehoshaphat. "This guy's terrible. Didn't I tell you he doesn't know how to prophesy anything good about me?"

Micaiah ignored Ahab's interruption and continued: "I saw the Lord sitting on his throne with the host of heaven around him. The Lord asked who would entice Ahab into attacking Ramoth Gilead so he would be killed there. After various suggestions, one spirit stood before the Lord and said he would entice Ahab. The Lord asked what means the spirit would use. The spirit said he would go out and be a lying spirit in the mouths of Ahab's prophets." Micaiah paused. "Listen to me, Ahab. The Lord has decreed disaster for you at Ramoth Gilead."

Zedekiah walked up and slapped Micaiah in the face and mocked him. Ahab stood up and ordered, "Put Micaiah in prison and give him nothing but bread and water until I return safely."

As they dragged Micaiah away, he declared, "If you return safely,

the Lord has not spoken through me. Mark my words, all you
people!"

Jehoshaphat received guidance from the Lord, but he decided to
ignore it and join Ahab in battle anyway. They went up to Ramoth
Gilead and a random arrow penetrated between the sections of
Ahab's armor. That evening he died and his army scattered, just as
Micaiah had prophesied (1 Kings 22:34–35; 2 Chron. 18:33–34).

When Jehoshaphat went home to Judah, God sent the prophet
Jehu with a message that God wasn't pleased with Jehoshaphat for
not obeying God's guidance and going to war with Ahab. But after
rebuking Jehoshaphat, Jehu said, "There is, however, some good in
you, for you have rid the land of the Asherah poles and have set
your heart on seeking God" (2 Chron. 19:3). Jehoshaphat had set
his heart on seeking God, and when he inquired of God to know
what to do, God answered through Micaiah. When he disobeyed,
God sent another prophet to admonish him. Jehoshaphat heard
God speak to him because he first set his heart on seeking God.

Even today we must still set our hearts on seeking God first before God will give us the guidance we ask for.

A Prayer Retreat to Get God's Guidance

David Knauss and his wife, Theresa, work in central Asia. David
has learned the effectiveness of prayer in their work. They had lived
in the country for one-and-a-half years, breaking new ground as
they sought to bring the gospel to this country. During that time,
not one person had believed. Overwhelmed, the team started what
they called their "Hour of Power," wherein the group got together
for one hour each week to pray for people in that country to know
Christ.

After three or four months of praying, God answered their prayers
when the first person believed. The men in the team would meet

for three-day prayer retreats. Instead of asking for anything, they would focus only on worship and praise. They would take a theme like the holiness of God and concentrate on it for hours, singing, praising, and focusing on God's holiness. Then they would move on to another attribute of God, such as his righteousness. After two-and-a-half days of seeking God's face and praising his name, the men would ask God what he wanted them to pray for. David says these times of prayer transformed his personal prayer life.

Now David leads another team in another village of the same country. As the leader, David felt a burden to be led by Christ in every decision he made. As he prayed, he felt a desire to see their ministry expand beyond the village to the whole southern region of the country. Then two churches from the United States offered to partner with David's team by providing extra workers and funds. From the circumstances it seemed God wanted the ministry to grow and this would be a good direction to go. When David sought the advice of others, they told him he should form a partnership program with these churches.

But David realized he had no clear word from God on the matter. He thus decided to spend time alone with God and ask God for guidance. He went to a home on the Oregon coast for a three-day personal retreat. David says, "I wanted to hear from God."

David knew waiting before the Lord meant just that—waiting. He began the first day in confession. He assumed it would take an hour or two and then he'd go on to ask the Lord for guidance. But as he allowed the Spirit to examine his heart, David felt broken before the Lord. God showed him things in his life that were not right, things like his attitudes and his finding rest and strength in areas other than God. David spent the whole first day, confessing and making things right with the Lord.

The second day David sat quietly before the Lord and waited. He read the Word and listened. But he heard nothing. He read sections from Randy Alcorn's book *Lord Foulgrin's Letters* (Multnomah, 2000), but David heard only silence during that second day.

By the third day David began to panic. He set aside three days to listen to the Lord and he hadn't gotten any guidance at all. He began that third day by having his regular quiet time from Isaiah 17:10–11, about how Israel cultivated beautiful plants and vines, yet in the end they would get no fruit because the people had forgotten the Lord their Savior.

As David looked at these verses, he saw there would be no fruit despite Israel's hard work in the fields, because God wasn't in their work. He asked himself whether God was in their plan to partner with these two churches. He prayed, "Lord, I guess if you're not in it, we shouldn't partner with these churches or there will be no fruit."

Still pondering whether he'd really received guidance from God, David saw his old leather-bound Bible. He hadn't been reading in this Bible for quite a while because he'd been using his One-Year Bible. Now he felt compelled to open the Bible. Tugging at the thin, ribbon bookmark, he flipped the Bible open and found himself looking at the story of Gideon in Judges 6. Verse 14 jumped out at him: "Go in the strength you have." When Gideon argued saying he wasn't worthy, God said, "I will be with you."

David felt as if God was speaking those very words to him: "Go and do it and I will be with you." He felt a sense of peace that God did want his team to partner with these churches for an expanded ministry. David then wrote down a list, outlining the vision he felt for this ministry. He even sensed God's desire for his family to move from the village into a city to open a development center with English classes, small business resources, and an orphanage.

As David prayed, God gave him a picture of going in and getting the approval of the elders of the city just as they'd done in their village. David also felt the Lord putting on his heart that if these churches wanted to partner, they should each be ready to invest $100,000 in the ministry. That figure seemed so large, it scared David, and he hesitated to tell anyone.

Later David talked with the churches and told them he felt that God wanted them to work together. The first church asked what kind of finances they would need to raise. David tried to hold back, but felt he had to speak out the amount God had told him. So he said $100,000. The first church did some calculations, and nodded. They felt they could invest that much in the project. David couldn't believe it. The other church didn't feel as sure, but felt they should go ahead and see whether the Lord could provide those finances.

A few weeks later on a trip back to central Asia to handle some other matters, David met with some of the government officials in the city where he felt they should start a new development center. The governor himself gave David an official invitation to work in that city, just as David had envisioned as he prayed.

God wants to show us the way, and he is ready to guide us. We have his Word. We have his Spirit in us, the very mind of Christ. David spent three days praying and asking the Lord for guidance, and God led him. We, too, need to take time to pray and ask for his wisdom, understanding, and guidance. One way of finding the time to discover God's guidance is by planning a personal prayer retreat and asking God for his leading.

three

BRINGING PRAYER BURDENS

Be pleased, O LORD, to save me; O LORD, come quickly to help me.

—Psalm 40:13

A THIRD REASON TO GO somewhere alone with God for a time of prayer is because we sense a heavy burden for some problem, and we want to ask the Lord to intercede in the situation or to provide for a specific need. The most common definition of prayer is asking God for something and he, in fact, wants us to ask. Jesus said, "Ask and it will be given to you; seek and you will find; knock and the door will be opened to you" (Matt. 7:7).

Asking God for help and for blessings is a very legitimate reason for praying. Even in other cultures, God is seen as the giver of blessings. According to the Maasai story of creation, when *Enkai* created the world, he put a rope between heaven and earth. Whenever the Maasai wanted anything, he went to the rope and asked God for blessings. God heard and sent cattle and goats down the rope.

Asking for Cowboy Pistols

I remember vividly the first time that God answered one of my prayers. I was in second grade and my best friend, Tim Wilson, and I loved to play cowboys. He came from Arizona and even had real cowboy boots. I wanted some guns—pistols I could wear in holsters strapped to my legs so I could practice drawing my weapons.

One day my Mom went to Nairobi on business. When I came home from school I thought, *If I pray, my Mom might buy me the guns I want.* I hid myself in the closet of the bedroom I shared with my brother Cam and prayed. In that dark closet, snuggled next to the dirty clothes basket, I sat on the floor and simply asked God to help my mother buy me some guns. In my mind, I wanted real guns that would shoot. I stayed in the closet, praying all afternoon.

Then I heard the door to the house open, and my Mom called out that she was home. I scrambled out of the closet and ran to see her. "You'll never guess what I bought for you in Nairobi!" she said.

"Guns," I answered, confident God had answered my prayer.

Mom looked a bit puzzled. "How did you guess?" she said, pulling out a set of cap guns in leather holsters. "I found these at a second-hand store, and I thought you'd like to play cowboys with them."

I burst with excitement. I had prayed for guns for several hours, and my Mom had bought me guns. It was amazing! True, I'd had in mind real guns with bullets, and now I had cap guns instead. But in my young mind I figured I'd forgotten to tell the Lord exactly what kind of guns I wanted. God had answered my prayer, selfish though it was, and given me safe toy guns.

That answered prayer helped me at a tender age to build my faith in a God, who hears and answers our prayers.

When We Don't Receive

Obviously asking shouldn't be our only reason for praying. Prayer that only asks becomes one-sided and self-centered. Even James noted this when he wrote, "When you ask, you do not receive, because you ask with wrong motives, that you may spend what you get on your pleasures" (James 4:3).

That's why we need to spend time in praising and honoring the Lord in our prayers. As we know him better, we will understand his heart, we will hear his voice, and we'll pray for the things God wants. We will pray according to God's will.

But there is nothing wrong with asking. We are weak, and God is strong. We are poor, and God is rich. Just before James told his readers they weren't receiving answers to their prayers because they were selfish, he pointed out another reason they were not receiving answers. He said, "You want something but don't get it. You kill and covet, but you cannot have what you want. You quarrel and fight. You do not have, because you do not ask God" (v. 2). Among other reasons, they didn't get anything because they weren't even praying. They weren't asking God for his help.

How can God answer when we don't pray? How can he give when we don't ask? God loves us and longs for us to come to him and pour our hearts out to him in prayer when we're burdened. He is *El Roi*, "God Who Sees" (see Gen. 16:13). He is the God who comes down and helps. And he is *El Shaddai*, "God Almighty," who can provide (see Ps. 111:4–8).

Hannah's Burden

Hannah punched another cake of cheese into the leather pouch. She didn't know if she could handle another trip with that preening co-wife Peninah and her brood of children. Even now the children ran in the courtyard, pushing and shoving and claiming their spots on the donkey's back. Hannah looked out the window. "O Lord, why can't I have at least one child? My barrenness might be easier to bear if Peninah didn't always rub it in. Lord, forgive me for that thought. I just don't think I can stand another day with the way she prides herself on all the children she has given to Elkanah. Lord, please give me a child, I pray."

Elkanah came in and put an arm around her shoulder. "Are you ready to go up and worship the Lord at Shiloh, my beloved?"

Hannah forced a smile. She did want to go and worship. She loved the Lord and wanted to take part in the yearly sacrifice. But she didn't like being surrounded by clear evidence of her own failure as a wife. She wanted to bring her own children to the Tent of Meeting to offer sacrifices to the Lord. She wanted Elkanah to give her and her own children pieces of the meat from the sacrifice.

Hannah knew Elkanah loved her. He always gave her a double portion of meat. But oh, the emptiness she felt as Elkanah gave Peninah chunks of meat for all her sons and daughters. And then the way Peninah carried her head pridefully as she herded her flock of children. It was just too much. "Lord, give me patience," Hannah breathed. "And while you're at it, please give me a son to take away my shame."

Hannah turned to Elkanah. "I'm just about ready," she said. "I just need to put in a few cakes of raisins for the children." And why isn't Peninah in here helping me pack the food? she thought bitterly. Her kids will devour most of it anyway.

At Shiloh, Elkanah worked with the priests Hophni and Phinehas to butcher the lamb he had brought as a fellowship offering of thanksgiving. Elkanah knew these two sons of Eli were scoundrels who tried to take the best portions of the sacrificial meat to eat for themselves. But Elkanah hovered over them to see they did everything properly. He laid his hand on the head of the lamb and slaughtered it at the entrance to the Tent of Meeting. Then he made sure the priests sprinkled the blood against the altar and on the sides.

Even as they cut up the lamb, Elkanah saw Hophni trying to take some of the uncooked fat. Elkanah blocked him. "All the fat is the Lord's," he said firmly. He then presented the priests with a cake of bread made without yeast, unleavened wafers spread with oil, cakes of fine flour mixed with oil, and cakes of bread made with yeast. They placed the meat of the sacrifices on the altar and the flame seared the meat, melting the fat, and scorching the air with the scent of burning meat.

After the fat had burned off and the meat was cooked, Elkanah brought portions of meat for each of his wives and Peninah's children. Even with her double portion, Hannah received far less than Peninah. "You'll notice how much meat Elkanah has given to me so that each of my children can take part in the fellowship and thanksgiving offering," Peninah declared, twisting the knife in Hannah's already bleeding heart.

The priests received their share, and Elkanah gathered his family together to share a communal meal and thank God for another good year.

Hannah began to weep quietly, her heart feeling like a cold stone within her. She couldn't eat the meat. Elkanah tried to comfort her. "Hannah, why are you weeping? Why don't you eat? Why are you downhearted? Don't I mean more to you than ten sons?"

Hannah turned away to hide her flow of tears. Yes, she loved Elkanah, but couldn't the Lord give her at least one son to take away her shame?

When the others finished eating and drinking, Hannah stood up and went to the Tent of Meeting. Ignoring Eli, the old priest who sat on a chair by the door of the tabernacle, Hannah crumpled down on her knees and in bitterness of soul began to pray. Tears flowed as she wept and pleaded with God for a son. As she beat down the doors of heaven with her request, she vowed to the Lord Almighty, "If you will only look on your servant's misery and remember me, and not forget your servant but give her a son, then I will give him to the Lord for all the days of his life."

In her misery and emptiness, Hannah continued to pray by the entrance of the Tent of Meeting. Eli shook his head as he watched Hannah pray with her eyes closed and lips moving silently. He knew the signs of a chronic drunkard. Eli walked toward her and scolded her: "How long will you keep on getting drunk? Get rid of your wine!"

Hannah, startled by this intrusion, looked up at the high priest through eyes reddened and swollen by her tears. "I am not drunk, my lord," she said. "I am a woman who is deeply troubled and I have been pouring my soul out to the Lord. Please don't think I'm a wicked woman. I haven't been drinking wine or beer. I have been praying here out of my great anguish and grief."

Eli wasn't used to people praying earnestly and wrestling for so long before the Lord. "Go in peace," he told her. "And may the God of Israel grant you what you have asked of him."

Hannah believed that God had answered her. She smiled at the priest and felt her burden lifting. She wiped her face with the sleeve of her robe, joined her family, and ate some food. Elkanah was delighted to see his wife looking happy again. "You look like my beloved wife again. What happened to change your grief?" he asked.

Hannah answered, "I prayed. I went to the Tent of Meeting and poured my soul out to the Lord and begged him for a son. I even promised the Lord that if he gave me a son, I would dedicate him to serve the Lord all his life. I feel within my heart that God will give me a son."

Elkanah loved Hannah and didn't want to crush her by reminding her of how many times they'd prayed before. But Hannah's face glowed. She had prayed through her burden and gained victory before the Lord. "Lord," Elkanah whispered, "may it be so. Reward Hannah for her faithfulness and prayers."

Soon Hannah did conceive and gave birth to a son. As Hannah nuzzled her newborn, she smiled at Elkanah and said, "I'm calling him Samuel because I asked the Lord for him and the Lord heard my prayer." Scripture's account of this story can be found in 1 Samuel 1.

God answered Hannah's prayer, for he loves to reach down and help his children when they cry out to him. To illustrate our need to be persistent in prayer, Jesus told the parable of the woman and the judge (Luke 18:1–8).

We can't manipulate God, figuring that if we take a day aside to pray about a particular prayer need, we'll see more answers than if we pray on the run. Prayer is an attitude of being humble before God and willing to accept his answer as we throw our needs at his feet.

It's not necessary to stop everything and take a day to pray. God answers prayers that are breathed in the midst of some problem. But when we are able to take extended time in prayer, it seems we are better able to see how powerful God is, and we're also better able to know God's heart about the matter. As a result, our prayers are more focused toward God's will, more earnest, and more effective.

God still answers prayer when we don't set aside large chunks of time to pray. But when we really feel the burden to prayer for a specific need, often the Lord will prompt us to spend a day or more focusing on that need.

A Burden for War-Torn Ethiopia

As fascist Italy began to flex its muscles before the start of World War II, Mussolini's army prepared to invade Ethiopia. Rees Howells, principal of a Bible school in Wales, looked on this threat of invasion with great sorrow. He felt a great burden for the country of Ethiopia. Howells felt that if the Italians gained control, it would sound the death knell of evangelical missions in that country. Howells took that burden and began to pray. He prayed specifically for Ethiopia to be delivered from Italy, and he led the students at his Bible college in Wales to pray.

On April 24, 1936, the school held a day of prayer and fasting. Feeling a great burden as they prayed for the Ethiopians, they believed the Italians would not enter Addis Ababa, the capital city. The next day they held four meetings of prayer. By April 28, they felt an even greater burden to pray for Ethiopia.

Thus, the fight for Ethiopia was fierce on the battlefield, and on the spiritual battlefield as well. The college journal records the school had spent "300 wonderful hours with the Lord pleading for the 100 missionaries in the capital."

The college set aside May 4 as another day of prayer and fasting. They felt a special burden for Addis Ababa as newspapers reported the rioting, which started when the emperor left the palace. On May 5, they still felt a burden to pray for Addis.

The Italian soldiers marched into the city at 4 P.M. that day.

Howells and his students had expected God to deliver Ethiopia from the Italians, but it didn't happen, in spite of all the hours in prayer. Howells and his students felt discouraged, feeling it would be the end of gospel work in Ethiopia. But after a time of prayer to sort out why God hadn't answered as they had hoped, Howells stood in front of the students and explained that apparent failure may only be the stepping stone to greater victory. Sometimes there had to be death in an intercession before there could be resurrection. He felt it was a test of the intercessors to see if they could keep their faith as they walked through a valley of humiliation at the apparent failure of their prayers.

Howells and his students at the Bible college never lost faith.

They continued to pray for Ethiopia. During the invasion, Emperor Haile Selassie I and his entourage fled to England as refugees. Later a missionary from Ethiopia asked Howells to take Lidj Asrate Kassa, one of the emperor's relatives, into a boarding school for missionary children operated by the college.

A year later, the emperor himself came to the college to visit Asrate and thanked Howells for his prayers on behalf of Ethiopia. The Emperor spent two weeks at the college and attended the nightly prayer meetings. Both the Emperor's private chaplain and son-in-law Abye Abebe studied at the Bible college.

In 1941, Italy was pushed out of Ethiopia, and Haile Selassie returned. He sent a cable to Howells thanking him for his sympathy and help. In the meantime, missionary work had greatly expanded in the country. When the missionaries returned to the Walemo area, they found that a revival had gone on during the Italian occupation. The number of believers had grown from five hundred to twenty thousand.

God answered the prayers of Howells and his students, although not exactly as they'd asked. But God knew the heart of their prayer was for a continued open door for the gospel. And following the Italian occupation, God did open up Ethiopia to greater penetration by the gospel.

Your Visas Are Denied

In 1999, David and Theresa Knauss needed their visas renewed so that they could continue to live and work in a central Asian country. They knew the officials fairly well and felt there would be no problem. But this time David met a new man in the office. After David requested a renewal of their visas, the man refused. "We don't want you here," the man said. "Go back home. Bye! Bye!"

David couldn't believe it! He began knocking on the doors of all the other government officials he knew. He tried every avenue and pushed every button for help, but failed.

It seemed an impossible situation. Without visas, they would have to leave the country. What more could they do to get the required visas? Then David realized with a jolt that he had been so busy trying to get help from other officials that he had neglected to pray. He spent a day fasting and praying and asking God to remove the roadblock and provide their visas, asking God to move in a way that they couldn't. David told God that he could do nothing more from human effort, and he left the problem at the Lord's feet.

After three weeks, David went back to the visa office. To his amazement he found that the official who had refused the visa renewal had been fired. Rarely are officials fired in this country. They are sometimes transferred, but not sacked. David and Theresa got the needed visas, and David thanked the Lord for the answer to his prayer. He felt as if God was saying, "I want you here! Don't forget, it's I who put you here."

David learned the importance of bringing prayer burdens to the Lord and taking a day to pray and fast over an unsolvable problem. God wants us to pray. When a burden or problem overwhelms us, we're in the best position possible. When we're defeated and unable to help ourselves, we're most likely to stop and take time to pray. God is pleased to answer and show his power. He wants us to ask. James wrote, "The prayer of a righteous man is powerful and effective" (5:16). More powerful prayer, however, often takes more time to effect.

When we feel a burden to pray for a specific need, it certainly is a good thing to set aside extended time to pray. Obviously we can't have a prayer retreat every time we feel a burden. We still need to pray every day and throughout our days as God brings needs to mind.

When faced with a problem or a heavy burden, we shouldn't get discouraged. Instead, we can use the problem as a lesson in learning to pray. We can set aside as much time as we can, come before God with our problem, pray, leave it with the Lord, and watch him answer.

PART TWO

WHAT TO DO ON A PRAYER RETREAT

WE DESIRE GOD. WE WANT TO spend time seeking his face. We want to know God better. We need his guidance, and we're desperate for his help. We want to have a prayer retreat, to spend a day in prayer.

But we're faced with that same question the young man asked me: *How do we do it?*

The second part of this book shows different things to do during a prayer retreat. No two people will organize a prayer day in the same way. I've talked with many people who have taken a day to pray, and each one does it differently. There is no formula for a prayer retreat, yet there are some prayer activities that most people include: praising God, confessing sins, thanking God, and reading and praying through Scripture. Some people fast, and others walk. Some memorize Scripture, listen to praise songs, and read devotional books, while others emphasize silence before God. Still others spend their prayer days listening to God. Part 2 looks at each of these aspects of prayer so that we can practice a variety of prayer activities when we plan our own prayer retreats.

One of my mentors in the area of personal prayer retreats is Dr. Jay Rupp. I got to know Jay when he worked as a missionary doctor at Kijabe Medical Center in Kenya. Each time I met Jay he invariably asked, "What are you doing to know the Lord better?" If I didn't have a good answer, I felt uncomfortable.

I began examining my life. Did I want to know God better? Jay organized a small group of men that met to spur one another to know God better. This grew into a group of men and women who prayed weekly for revival in that area of Kenya. In his quest for God, Jay would book prayer days into his busy schedule as a missionary physician. It's from him that I learned the importance of personal prayer retreats. Jay describes how he would spend a day in prayer during his time in Kenya.

One Man's Prayer Retreat

I asked Jay about his prayer retreats for this book. His response follows:

> The best prayer times for me while living in Africa have been when I escaped the world and my hectic schedule as a physician at a mission hospital and went to Burch's Camp on Lake Naivasha. I took my four-man tent and disappeared from the world and carved out a quiet space for just me and the Lord to be together. My retreats would start when I drove out of the driveway of our home and end when I drove back in at night and turned the car off. I would invite the Lord to join me in a close, personal way. I would even ask him to sit in the empty car seat next to me so we could see the sights together and chat as we traveled to and from the camp.
>
> What happens on a prayer retreat is a bit out of my con-

trol. I try to share ownership of the day with the Lord right at the outset. I can set my plans and I have different options for how I desire to spend my time, but the day also belongs to the Lord. I invite him to direct my thoughts and guide where we go on the prayer safari. Each time is different, and where we go spiritually is generally a new experience each time.

I pitch my tent and generally leave the flap down. I'm closed down. It's just me and the Lord. I lay out my mattress, lots of pillows, my sleeping bag, and a cooler. I find it's good to have a comfortable folding camp chair set up as well. Lying down all day can be uncomfortable.

I never fast on a prayer day. I usually fast a day or two before, and specifically focus that fasting on being in the Lord's presence on my upcoming prayer day. I bring food that I will savor—fruit, nuts, brownies, jerky, juice or soda, sandwiches with lots of goodness inside, and chips. I see my times with the Lord as a date, a special celebration together, and I want the Lord to enjoy the food too, because he lives within me!

Deal with Sin

Sin wrecks any attempt to be close to God. Deal thoroughly with sin. If there's sin that needs to be dealt with, I do it before or at the beginning of my retreat with the Lord. I confess any sins and am totally forgiven using the promise from 1 John 1:9, "If we confess our sins, he is faithful and just and will forgive us our sins and purify us from all unrighteousness."

I bring my Bible, my diary, and any books that I think would be helpful for centering on God and listening to him.

This isn't a time for me to study, or work on a devotional, or accomplish a task. It's a special date with the Lord and I want to be open to what he says. For me, that involves significant silence. I realize I can invite the Lord to be with me, but I can't force him to come. My plan is to place myself along the path where the Lord often walks. If he comes by on the path, I'll be there. I can't demand his presence or his voice.

As I begin, the struggles and lists of things that I should be doing instead of having a silent retreat prayer day buzz around in my head, distracting me from God. I have to jettison all the junk, and dump all the irons I have in the fire that are part of my daily life. I just write them on a piece of paper. I don't have to deal with them then; and once I've written them down, I can forget about them during the day. I'll pick up the list after I turn the car off in the driveway when my day with the Lord is done.

Devotions and Scripture

First I have my normal devotions and quiet time. Then I just pray for all the things that need to be prayed for. There is no rush. It's just good to max out on praying for everything that needs to be prayed for and to be topped off in that area.

Fatigue and sleep are not the enemies of prayer days. If I get too sleepy, I just sleep. I generally don't sleep for more than an hour or two, and even if this happens once or twice during the day, it's best to be rested and just give the Lord thanks for such a luxury. We all tend to be sleep deprived. Plan on sleeping so you don't feel guilty when you sleep for part of your prayer day.

After I finish my normal daily devotions, I read a book of the Bible. Matthew is my favorite book. I just get comfortable and read the whole book, having asked the Lord to speak to me through it. I read leisurely, lingering over passages where it seems the Lord is speaking to me. There is lots of time. I have a whole day. I invite the Lord to sit in the chair next to me. This is a special guys time together and I talk out loud to the Lord, but I have to be a bit sensitive to anyone who might be walking past the tent.

After reading the Bible, I might read from some other book. I enjoy Richard Foster's book *Prayer* (London: Hodder and Stoughton, 1992), especially the chapters on listening to God. Blackaby's book *Experiencing God* (Broadman & Holman, 1994) is good. Ignatius' Protestant version retreat stuff (including *Ignatian Method of Prayer* by Alexandre Bron (Milwaukee: Bruce, 1949); *The Spiritual Exercises of St. Ignatius* translated by Anthony Mottola (New York: Doubleday, 1964); and *Devotional Classics* edited by Richard J. Foster and James Bryan Smith (New York: HarperSanFrancisco, 1993) have helped me as well.

Praise the Lord

I read for a while to focus on the Lord and then I start to praise God. I am firmly convinced that the highest form of human activity we can indulge in—far greater than witnessing or other good works—is praising God. I love to read Revelation 4 and meditate on that picture of God's throne, putting myself right there with John, awed by God's majesty. Putting my mind in a holding pattern of praise, honor, glory, and worship, pleases the Lord.

But even as I meditate and pray, I find my mind wandering.

It occurs hundreds of times during a prayer day, and I've realized it's OK and normal. I just tell the Lord, "Sorry, I got lost briefly. But I'm back again." Then I resume where I left off. If your mind daydreams one-quarter of the time, thank the Lord for the fact that you spent three-quarters of the time together with the Lord. And just add a couple of hours to your retreat!

The time generally goes so fast and at the same time, so, so slowly. It is luxurious to have a whole day with the Lord. I savor its slowness. I have my diary close by and try to write down any thoughts that seem to hit home. I don't want to forget anything the Lord seems to be saying to me.

Listen to God

At some point during the day, I finally finish praying for all I want to pray about and finish reading as much as I can absorb. This is the best time of the retreat. I have nothing more to add or say or read! It's time to be still and know that the Lord is God. This is a wonderful benchmark time to reach in a silent retreat. This is the time to listen spiritually.

Maybe I'll hear nothing—that is what we all fear when we stop talking and just remain silent. My mind wanders and I return and listen some more. I remember that Jesus said, "My sheep hear my voice" (John 10:27 KJV), and I listen. I can't force the Lord to speak, but I've learned to wait patiently and expectantly.

God eventually does speak and honors my desire to come closer and hear his voice. I have to keep alert. He speaks in many different ways. Sometimes it's through Scripture, and at other times it's with his still small voice. Listening to God takes practice. The more I've practiced, the closer he seems and the more I've heard. It's like God is fulfilling his promise from James 4:8, one of my favorite verses: "Come near to God and he will come near to you."

And that's why I schedule prayer retreats. I want to get closer to God.

four

PRAISING GOD THROUGH THE PSALMS

Sing the glory of his name; make his praise glorious!
—Psalm 66:2

THE BEST PLACE TO START A DAY of prayer is by praising the Lord. Praise means to honor God and lift up his name because of who he is. Praise looks at God's character. We can fill our lips with praise by looking at the Psalms and other sections of the Bible that focus on praising God.

A Big Picture of God

By starting with praise, we gain a new perspective on how great God is. When we spend time praising God for his power, his strength, his holiness, his love, his ability to hear our prayers, his desire to help his people, his compassion, his mercy, and more, our picture of God grows. "O magnify the LORD with me, and let us exalt his name together," David wrote in Psalm 34:3 (KJV). The

Hebrew word translated *magnify* literally means to make something large by twisting together many small threads. We magnify the Lord and make his name big as we mention all the threads that make up his character. *Exalt* means to lift up and make high. David urges us to join him in praising God by making his name huge and lifting his name high. We do it by our individual praises.

Praise helps us get our focus right. As we praise God and keep adding strands of praise, we end up with a magnificent picture of God. We realize that since God is so great, he is certainly able to handle the prayer needs I'm bringing before him. Praising God, magnifying his name, and exalting him puts things in proper perspective.

If we skip over the step of praise, it's easy to be overwhelmed by our needs. We come to pray and begin listing our litany of problems. The heap grows higher and higher, and pretty soon we begin to suffocate under the weight of our own needs.

I work with twenty young churches in Kenya, and the needs are great. I feel like Paul in 2 Corinthians 11:28: "Besides everything else, I face daily the pressure of my concern for all the churches." If I only look at the needs at one of our weekly team prayer meetings, I can become discouraged. That's because I often forget to praise the Lord first.

When I take time to praise the Lord and magnify his name, I find I'm overwhelmed by God's power. As my picture of God grows larger at the beginning of my prayer time, it affects how I approach God with my needs. If God had the power to raise Jesus from the dead, surely he has the power to change the heart of that person who has fallen back into a life of sin.

Prayer times that begin with proper praise end up being colored with optimism. There isn't a mountain high enough to keep God from building his kingdom in my heart and in the lives of others. I'm not saying this is a way to avoid the seriousness of our needs and problems. But as we seriously praise God for who he is, then he's lifted high and his name is magnified. The mountain that is our God is a lot higher than the dung heap of our needs.

When we praise God, he is overjoyed and pleased by our praises. Paul wrote in Ephesians 1:3–12 that we are created and redeemed for the praise of his glory. That's why God made us. He wants us to praise him.

And praise is humbling. As we realize how holy God is, it should send us to our knees in confession, especially as we ask forgiveness for our own prideful, selfish, "I can do it myself" lifestyles. When we build a proper regard for God by our praise, we know how far we are from the glory of God. It puts us in the proper position for confession, and for praying out of dependence on our awesome, comparison-defying God. Praise reminds us and teaches us more about our God as we take time to lift praise up to God, the Creator of the universe, for his amazing character.

How to Use a Psalm to Praise God

The Psalms are songs and poems dedicated to praising God. Many of the things the psalmists wrote are similar because the songs were written about the same God. But often a songwriter noted something from a new perspective. We can start almost anywhere in the Psalms.

Look at Psalm 34, for example. The easiest way to start is to read the psalm out loud, just as it's written. Psalm 34 is written in first person, so it's easy to put yourself in the place of David and praise God as he did at a difficult time when his life was in danger and he pretended to be insane to escape from the Philistine King Abimelech. After reading through the psalm out loud once or twice, read it again, using a pencil or marker to note everything David praises God for.

The first three verses talk about extolling, praising, glorifying, and exalting the Lord's name. Then in verse 4 we could underline "he answered me" and "he delivered me from all my fears." As we turn these facts about what God has done into our own prayer of praise, we could pray, "I praise you, Lord, and exalt your name. I praise you because you answer my prayers. I praise you because you deliver me from all my fears. I praise you, God, that you are a deliverer."

Verse 5 speaks of the frame of mind of those who pray rather than any characteristics of God, but we could still praise the Lord like this: "I praise you, God, that, when I look at you, I am radiant. I praise you that my radiance is a reflection of your brilliance. I praise you, Lord, that, when I pray to you, I'll never be ashamed, because you answer the prayers of your people."

In verses 6 and 7, we could underline "The LORD heard him; he saved him out of all his troubles. The angel of the LORD encamps around those who fear him, and he delivers them." In response, one might praise the Lord like this:

O Lord, I praise you because you hear my prayer when I call out. Even if I am poor and needy, you hear. I praise you, God, for having big ears. No plea is too small for you to hear. I praise you that you have the power to save those who call upon you. No matter how big the trouble is, you are greater and more powerful. I praise you that you send your angel to encamp around me. I praise you for being a God of protection. And again, O Lord, I praise you for being a God who delivers.

In verses 8–10, we could underline "the LORD is good," "refuge," and "lack no good thing" twice. Then we could praise God like this:

I praise you, God, because you are good. You are completely good. There is no sin, no blemish in you. You are all good. I praise you for your goodness. I praise you, Father God, because you are a refuge. I can run to you and be safe. I praise you for being a safe place to hide. I praise you, Father, because you provide everything. If I fear you, if I seek you, I will lack nothing. I praise you, God, for being the One who provides every good thing. You are my provider.

Verses 11–14 focus on how we should live. But in verses 15 and 16 we could underline "The eyes of the LORD are on the righteous, and his ears are attentive to their cry" and "the LORD is against those who do evil." Our praise from these verses might go like this:

I praise you, Lord, because your eyes see everything and you are looking down on your people. I praise you that you see me right now where I am. I praise you as well because your ears are attentive. Your ears are quick to hear. I praise you that you are able to hear my cry. And I praise you, God, because you are against evil doers. Sometimes it seems like evil is winning in this world. Satan seems to be so in control. I praise you for this reminder that you are against those who do evil. I praise you because you will win the battle against evil and sin.

In verses 17 and 18, we could underline "The LORD hears them; he delivers them. . . . The LORD is close to the brokenhearted and saves those who are crushed in spirit." Our praise built out of these verses could resound:

I am amazed, Lord, that you hear the cry of the righteous. I praise you because you are a hearing God. And I praise you because, when you hear, you act and you deliver the righteous from all their troubles. I praise you, Father, that you can hear my prayers today and that you're just as ready to deliver me now from my troubles as you were to deliver David from the Philistines. I praise you, Lord, because you are close to the brokenhearted. I've come with a broken heart today. I hurt so badly. I praise you because you are not only a high and mighty powerful deliverer, but you are also a comforting God who is close. I praise you because you save the ones whose spirits have been crushed.

In verses 19–22, we could underline "the Lord delivers," "he protects," "the Lord redeems," and "no one will be condemned who takes refuge in him." We may feel like we've praised God for being a deliverer too many times already, but God doesn't get tired of hearing our praises. He doesn't say, "Hold on, I've heard that one." No, God wants us to praise him.

When David wrote this psalm, he needed deliverance, so he mentioned God's delivering power over and over. As we praise the Lord, we can mention it over again as well.

O Lord, I praise you as the One who delivers. No other has power like you to save. I praise you, Father, because you are a protector. I praise you that you protect every one of my bones. I praise you that you redeem the ones who run to you. You pay for our deliverance. I praise you because you don't condemn the ones who run to you for refuge. I praise you for being a merciful God.

These are prayers I might use and are not meant for everyone to follow. But they show how we can use one psalm to be reminded of a lot of things about God and his character that are worthy of our praise.

As we use the Psalms as a basis for our praise, we won't all see the same things I mentioned in this example. As we pray and ask the Lord to reveal things about himself as we read the Psalms, he will show us aspects of his character. Then we can stop and pray them back to God as praise.

Listen to Praise Songs

Another way to praise the Lord is by listening to songs and hymns. Many recordings of worshipful praise songs are available. We can choose some praise music we like and set a time during our prayer day to listen and worship God through those praise songs. We can even sing along with the music, but we have to choose our place to sing carefully. Once I used a small tape recorder and earphones to listen to some worship songs. As I lay on my bed, singing along with the music, my wife heard the noise and walked in. She couldn't figure out why I was singing away by myself. Since then I've been careful to sing along to praise music only when I'm alone in the house.

As we praise the Lord through prayer and song, we'll find we are magnifying the Lord's name. Our picture of God's greatness and power will grow, and we'll pray more confidently as we approach our God, whom we now know better because we took the time to praise his name.

Praise-Filled Passages of Scripture

We can use almost any psalm and pull out praiseworthy things about God. My old Bible has little green markings all through the book of Psalms where I've underlined attributes of God I can use to praise him. That way whenever I need to stop and praise God, I just open the Psalms and start praising God for the things I've underlined. Some psalms in my Bible are almost completely underlined in green. They're brimming over with praise to the God we serve.

Here's a list of some psalms and other Scriptures that will be especially useful when praising God during a prayer day. Many more passages can be used to guide our time of praise, but these provide a good starting place.

- Exodus 15:1–18
- Psalm 19
- Psalm 23
- Psalm 29
- Psalm 33
- Psalm 47
- Psalm 65
- Psalm 68
- Psalm 89
- Psalm 91
- Psalm 93
- Psalm 96
- Psalm 103
- Psalm 104
- Psalm 111
- Psalm 121
- Psalm 139
- Psalm 145
- Psalm 146
- Psalm 148
- Isaiah 6:1–7
- Isaiah 53
- Revelation 4
- Revelation 7:11–17

five

CONFESSING OUR SINS

Then I acknowledged my sin to you and did not cover up
my iniquity. I said, "I will confess my transgressions to the
LORD"—and you forgave the guilt of my sin.

—Psalm 32:5

AFTER A GOOD SESSION OF PRAISE, we should feel humbled. As we recite
God's holiness, we should fall on our face in confession asking God
to forgive us. Thus, praise is best followed by a time of confession.

Isaiah Sees God's Holiness

Isaiah fell to the ground in terror (Isa. 6:1–7). He had just seen
the Lord, and his whole body trembled with fear. As Isaiah had
been in prayer and seeking God's face, the Lord appeared to him.
He saw the Lord seated on his throne, which dominated the temple
with its high and exalted position. The Lord's robe filled the temple,
and seraphs—six-winged angels—flew in front of the Lord's presence. Their voices boomed out, "Holy, holy, holy is the LORD Almighty; the whole earth is full of his glory" (v. 3).

69

Isaiah cupped his palms around his ears as the angels' voices shook the door posts and the thresholds of the temple. Smoke shrouded the sanctuary. Isaiah wanted to escape. He knew he didn't deserve to stand in the presence of his holy God. "Woe to me!" Isaiah cried out. "I am ruined! For I am a man of unclean lips, and I live among a people of unclean lips, and my eyes have seen the King, the Lord Almighty" (v. 5).

Praise Leads to Confession

Often a session of praise leads right into a time of confession. As Isaiah realized how holy, sinless, and perfect God is, he fell down and confessed that he was a man of unclean lips. He was a sinner living in a sinful world. God reached out and sent a seraph to Isaiah with a live coal taken with tongs from the altar. The angel touched it to Isaiah's lips and assured Isaiah that his sins had been paid for and his guilt had been taken away (Isa. 6:6–7). When we confess our sinfulness, God does forgive us and he allows us into his presence.

During praise, we also see how sinful we are. I don't mean just the obvious sinful actions we can remember, but attitudes that show we are not putting God first in our lives—pride, selfishness, jealousy, anger, and self-reliance: "I can do it myself, God. I don't need you." Also included are lack of prayer and the greed of putting things and possessions ahead of God. And there are so many more obstacles between God's holiness and my sinfulness.

Nothing is more essential to effective prayer than a time of confession. The reason confession is so important is that it puts us in a humble position before God. We realize our own need of God and our own sinfulness. Then, as we confess, he is ready and willing to forgive us and cleanse us from all of our sins. God hears prayers from a purified heart.

The Bible is clear that if we harbor sin in our hearts, God does not hear our prayers. "If I had cherished sin in my heart, the Lord would not have listened; but God has surely listened and heard my voice in prayer" (Ps. 66:18–19). The psalmist knows that if he cherished, or loved, and refused to give up, certain sins, the Lord would not listen to his prayer. But God has listened. Why? Because the psalmist confessed his sins.

Unconfessed sin not only hinders our prayers but also is unhealthy. When we keep silent about our sins and hope God doesn't notice, it tears us up inside. David tried to cover up his sin and wrote about it in Psalm 32:3–6: "When I kept silent, my bones wasted away through my groaning all day long. For day and night your hand was heavy upon me; my strength was sapped as in the heat of summer. Then I acknowledged my sin to you and did not cover up my iniquity. I said, 'I will confess my transgressions to the LORD'—and you forgave the guilt of my sin. Therefore let everyone who is godly pray to you while you may be found."

A Second-Grade Sin

I covered up a sin for over a year when I was in second grade. And I experienced the heavy hand of guilt and the rubbery legs of fear as I waited for someone to discover what I'd done. It wasn't a big sin at first.

I dawdled. My mom would become exasperated, getting me out of the house and on the way to Rift Valley Academy where I was in Miss Cook's class. One morning I dawdled more than usual while getting dressed and eating breakfast, and by the time my mom pushed me out the front door I heard the first bell ringing. That meant I had five minutes to be in my seat, and it was a ten-minute hike uphill. I began to run, but halfway up the hill I heard the second bell ring. I was late. I didn't want to walk into class late so I decided to jump into a ditch and hide there. I hid in the ditch all morning. Just before noon I heard the bell ring for the end of school, and I walked home for lunch. My hands trembled and my stomach hurt as I walked into the house. I was sure my mom would somehow know I'd played hooky that morning.

"Did you remember to bring home that sweater from school?" my Mom asked.

I gulped. "No, I forgot to look for it," I lied. Did she know I was lying?

I went to school in the afternoon. I didn't know what to tell Miss Cook about missing the morning classes. But as I walked in, she smiled: "Shelly, were you feeling sick this morning? I hope you're feeling better now."

"Oh, yes, I'm feeling much better now," I answered. I hadn't really lied, I told myself. She thought I was sick. I didn't say I was. And I really did feel better because she'd given me an excuse for not being in school that morning, and I hadn't gotten into trouble.

That night I could hardly sleep. I kept expecting Miss Cook and my mom to compare notes and realize I had never gone to school that morning. But days and then weeks went by. Nobody knew. I'd committed the perfect crime. But it tore me up inside. I knew I'd done something wrong and then lied to cover it up. Every time we had family devotions, I knew I should confess what I'd done, but I always chickened out. And God's hand remained heavy upon me.

Finally, a year later, I could stand it no longer. I couldn't sleep, my face felt hot. I knew I had to confess. I went to my Mom's bed and told her what I'd done and asked her to forgive me. I fully expected punishment. But to my surprise, my Mom forgave me. Then she said if I'd had a guilty conscience for a year, I'd already suffered enough. I thanked her and thanked the Lord, then I went to bed, feeling forgiven and lighthearted. My sin had been forgiven. But I'd had to carry it for a year until I was ready to confess and ask for forgiveness.

King David Covers Up

King David paced around on the roof of his palace. He'd sent his soldiers out to fight against the Ammonites. David had decided to stay home from this military campaign. General Joab could handle it. David had to think about other things, matters of state. Now his mind buzzed with advice from his counselors about consolidating the kingdom and protecting the boundaries by treaties. David shook his head, trying to clear it. "I'd be better off on the battlefield," he muttered to himself.

A shadow on a nearby rooftop caught David's eye. He looked down and saw a woman bathing. She was beautiful. He called a servant. "Go find out what woman lives in that house," David commanded.

The man reported back, "The woman is Bathsheba, wife of Uriah the Hittite, one of your soldiers." David sent messengers to bring the woman to him, and he slept with her before sending her back home. David hoped no one would know what he had done. He kept silent, but in his heart he felt the burden of his sin. He felt drained, without strength.

The woman conceived and sent word to David. "I am pregnant." David sweated as he thought, *Now what do I do? Uriah's been on the battlefield, and he'll know someone else laid with his wife.* But instead of confessing his sin, David sent messengers to bring Uriah back from the battlefield.

David met the man and tried to persuade Uriah to go home and spend the night with his wife. Then, when Bathsheba's baby would be born, Uriah wouldn't suspect it was someone else's child. Born a trifle early, maybe. But Uriah refused to go home. He slept at the palace gate.

David, barely able to control his anger, asked why Uriah hadn't gone home to spend the night with Bathsheba. Uriah said he couldn't possibly relax at home, and eat and drink and lie with his wife while the rest of the army was out camped in the fields.

David felt as if a knife sliced through his heart. But he tried again. That night he sat with Uriah and gave him wine and food and insisted Uriah eat and drink until he was drunk. But even in his drunkenness, Uriah didn't go home.

Desperate to cover his sin, David wrote a letter to Joab, general of the army. The letter asked Joab to put Uriah in the front line where the fighting would be fiercest, and then to withdraw the other men, leaving Uriah to be killed. David felt that the only way to cover up his sin was to kill Uriah.

Joab obeyed the instructions and Uriah was killed in battle. Joab sent a letter to David stating the deed had been done. To cover up his adultery, David had ordered Uriah's murder. Yet he still did not confess his sin. He took Bathsheba to be his wife and she had a son.

All along, David's soul shriveled as he tried to live a lie, covering up his sin. God sent the prophet Nathan to rebuke him.

As David listened to Nathan's accusation, his heart melted. He confessed, "I have sinned against the Lord." Nathan immediately reassured him, "The Lord has taken away your sin."

When we confess, God does take away our sin; he does forgive us. That doesn't mean sin has no consequences. Nathan told David that his son from the union with Bathsheba would die and there would be fighting and killing within David's house for the rest of his life as a result of David's sin.

But as soon as David confessed his sin, God forgave him, and David could once again pray and talk with God.

David wrote Psalm 51 after Nathan confronted him about his adultery with Bathsheba and the murder of Uriah. From David's confession, we can learn how to take time to confess our sins as well.

In Psalm 51, David begins by citing God's mercy, unfailing love, and compassion. "I know I've sinned, God," David prays. "I deserve judgment. Don't forget that you are a merciful, loving, compassionate God." Then David asks God to blot out his transgressions, wash away his iniquity, and cleanse him from his sin.

Despite his sin, David knows God is merciful and loving and ready to forgive him. And David is willing to call his actions sin. He doesn't try to fudge or rename his sins as something else. He calls his actions transgressions, iniquity, and sin. Then he goes on to say he knows his transgressions, and he confesses that he has sinned against God and done evil in God's sight.

Later David confesses his very sin nature, saying he was sinful at birth, sinful from the time his mother conceived him. Then David asks God to cleanse him, to wash him. David is confident that God is able to forgive and also to cleanse him and make him whiter than snow. David asks that his crushed bones (caused by hiding his sin) would rejoice and he would hear joy and gladness. He asks God to hide his face from David's sins, and again calls on God to blot out his iniquity.

David then asks the Lord to create a pure heart in his inner being. He asks for a renewed, steadfast spirit and begs not to be thrown away from God's presence. David felt so alone when he lived away from God's presence while he tried to cover up his sin. He begs to be returned to God's presence, asking that the Holy Spirit not be taken from him. And he asks the Lord to restore to him the joy of his salvation and for a willing spirit to sustain him.

David knows the forgiveness of God as he confesses his sin. He writes that he will teach others to turn from sin, and his lips will praise the Lord because the Lord saved him "from bloodguilt" (Ps. 51:14). David says no amount of animal sacrifice will please God. But the sacrifice God wants is a broken spirit, and a broken and contrite heart.

Search Our Hearts, Lord

As we begin a time of confession during a prayer retreat, we should start by asking the Lord to search our hearts and show us if there is some evil way in us. David had committed an obvious sin by committing adultery and then murdering Uriah. But he rationalized his sin and hid it as best he could. When Nathan confronted him, David broke right away and asked for forgiveness.

But there are times when attitudes, thoughts, bitterness, anger, and other things creep into our hearts almost without our realizing it. We may sit down to confess our sins and think, *I don't have too much to confess. I'm doing pretty good. I'm in church on Sundays . . . well, most of the time. I haven't committed adultery. I haven't killed anyone.*

We're like an old Dorobo man I met one day in the highland forest of Kenya. I shared the gospel with him, and he listened to what I had to say. He said he'd be happy to pray and confess his sins so he could have salvation in Jesus Christ. But he wanted me to know he really didn't have any sins to confess as he hadn't sinned in over twenty years. Since he hadn't killed anyone in the past twenty years, he hadn't sinned. He had a much narrower view of sin than God did.

According to God, sin is missing the mark and not reaching God's holy standard. Whether it's something we've done or something we've forgotten to do, we have all missed the mark.

Have we gotten angry? Jesus said that improper anger deserves judgment as much as murder. Maybe we haven't committed adultery, but have we experienced lust as we looked at images on the TV screen? If so, Jesus said we've committed adultery in our hearts. John put it this way: "If we claim to be without sin, we deceive ourselves and the truth is not in us" (1 John 1:8). Sometimes by ignoring sins or claiming our sinful actions are somehow justified, we live in a deceived state that we have no sins to confess.

I remember studying under Dr. John Mitchell from Multnomah School of the Bible. As I looked at this aging saint whose love for the Lord oozed out of his every word, teaching us the epistles of Paul and quoting long sections of Scripture by heart, I thought how godly he was. Yet he told us that as he got to know the Lord better, the more he realized how sinful he was.

Our knowledge and understanding of our sinfulness grows as we learn to understand the absolute holiness of God and his character. Never in this body can we say, "Well, I have nothing to confess today. I did pretty well so I won't have to bother God with a confession today."

Confess Our Sins

Take time alone to confess. Sit quietly before God, and pray, as David did: "Search me, O God, and know my heart; test me and know my anxious thoughts. See if there is any offensive way in me, and lead me in the way everlasting" (Ps. 139:23–24). As we pray and ask God to search our hearts, he will bring things into our minds. As he does, we need to pray and agree with the Lord that we have sinned in specific thoughts and actions. We must confess these as sin and ask the Lord to forgive us and cleanse us from such transgressions, praying to receive strength to stand firm in these areas.

Each of these sins that God reveals is hindering our relationship with him. We must remember that Christ carried the guilt of each sin on his body while he hung on the cross. We should thank him for his sacrifice for our sins, praying and letting the blood of Christ wash away our sin. Remember God's promise: "If we confess our sins, he is faithful and just and will forgive us our sins and purify us from all unrighteousness" (1 John 1:9).

As we finish dealing with one area of failure, we ask God to show us something else. If it's been a while since we've taken time for deep, cleansing confession, this may take hours—maybe even the full day.

I remember one of the first times we took a day to pray. I spent a long time in confession. As I looked back at my life, God prompted me to remember many things I'd done back in high school and college. I hadn't ever taken an extended time to examine my life. It was humbling. I had to ask some people for forgiveness. Other things were so far past I couldn't find those people again. But the Lord assured me that as I confessed my sins against him, he forgave me.

David's adultery and murder hurt and betrayed many. Yet he prayed to God, "Against you and you only have I sinned." Where we can ask someone's forgiveness, we should do it. But if it's not possible, we can release that sin and trust in God's forgiveness.

Bury Forgiven Sin

It is important for us to bury sins once we've confessed them. David wrote, "As far as the east is from the west, so far has he removed our transgressions from us" (Ps. 103:12).

We don't need to go back and confess the same sins over and over. Once a sin has been confessed and forgiven, the Lord has taken it away. If we have completed the process of working through a particularly troubling sin, and experience further prodding in our hearts about that sin, the urging may not come from the Lord. Rather, it may be Satan, the Accuser, nudging and saying, "How can you be a Christian? Don't you remember the time you committed adultery? What a faithless man you are. What a hypocrite you are to think you can be an example to others. Who do you think you are pretending you're a child of God?"

When Satan brings up past failings that have been confessed and forgiven, we should stand firm against him. We can proclaim the truth that even though we have sinned, the blood of Jesus covers us, and God the Father sees us as righteous because of what Christ did at the cross.

If our first time of deep confession takes a long time, even all day, we shouldn't worry. True confession brings healing and rebuilds our relationship with God. It needs to be completed before going on to prayer. If our first prayer day gets no further than confession, it will be a life-changing meeting with God as we realize how much junk we've been carrying around.

Parable of the Littered Roadside

The path I run each morning takes me alongside a busy road. One morning I found the roadside littered with newspapers. Apparently some newspaper carrier had dropped a bundle of newspapers out of the car. The wind had scattered them, leaving the roadside disheveled.

I stopped to pick up the newspapers, and as I did, I also noticed some cans, fast food wrappers, and other litter. I decided to pick those up as well. And as I picked up other loose junk, I found even more things embedded in the dirt—broken bottles, scraps of metal, and more. I carried away three armfuls of garbage that morning, and still more was left out there. Now I pick up a few small things on every run, and the roadside gets cleaner every day.

It's the same way with sin. Sometimes we don't bother to confess our sins until something big and obvious comes up, like the newspapers blowing along the roadside. But as we take time to deal with the obvious sin, we find that our life is cluttered with all sorts of other refuse that needs to be rooted out. The first few times of confession are a bit rough, as we gather up garbage sacks full of sin, confess them to God, and accept his forgiveness.

Once we are free from the burden of unconfessed sins, we will be able to pray, and God will hear our requests. In the future, we'll only need to confess our sinful attitudes and actions since our last time of confession. And if we build confession into our regular daily devotions, this session on a prayer retreat will probably become shorter as we learn to keep current by confessing sins regularly.

If the Lord brings tears during this time of confession, then weep. God wants us to have a broken heart and a broken spirit before him. He wants us to realize how much we need him and how often our sinful nature leads us to try to live the Christian life in our own power.

Prayer is talking with God. It shows we have a relationship with God, a friendship with the eternal Creator because of Christ's work on the cross. We can't have that fellowship—that intimate conversation with God that is true prayer—when we have unconfessed sin in our lives. Sin always cuts us off from our holy God.

Peter also said that when a husband doesn't treat his wife with proper respect, this hinders our prayers (1 Peter 3:7). Poor relationships caused by our sinful selfishness keep our prayers ineffective. Confession is the only way to forgiveness, to righting our relationship with God and with those we live with. Once sins are confessed and dealt with, we'll be able to talk with God. We'll be able to pray effectively.

Sometimes it helps to read and see how others have confessed and prayed for forgiveness before God. Analyze Daniel 9:4–19 and Nehemiah 1:4–11 as we have broken down the elements of Psalm 51. These three prayers of confession are good models and each has its own points to use in times of confession.

six

THANKING ALWAYS

Save us, O LORD our God, and gather us from the nations, that we may give thanks to your holy name and glory in your praise.

—Psalm 106:47

EVERY PRAYER RETREAT SHOULD include a time of giving thanks to God. Thanksgiving and praise are often interchanged, but where praise refers to God's goodness, his attributes, and his character, thanksgiving speaks of God's specific actions. When we thank God, we remember what he has done for us and for others in the past. And we simply say "Thank you." When we don't give thanks, we quickly forget what God has done, which can lead to the judgment of God. An African folk tale illustrates what happens when we forget to be thankful.

The Ungrateful Squirrel

Long, long ago, a squirrel and a lion became the best of friends. The lion invited the squirrel to share the protection of his den and gave the little squirrel leftover scraps of meat after he went hunting. In exchange, the squirrel tidied the den and kept everything nice for the lion.

But after a while the squirrel began to feel sorry for himself. The lion got to go out on exciting hunting expeditions while the squirrel stayed home sweeping and dusting. The lion got the biggest share of the meat—"the lion's share"—while the squirrel only got the scraps. The squirrel forgot all the benefits he received because of their friendship. He forgot about having a safe, snug cave to live in. He forgot about the years before he'd met the lion when he'd often experienced gnawing, gut-tightening hunger. Even though the squirrel ate meat scraps, he always had food. The squirrel forgot about all the good things he had and began to dream about what he didn't have. He thought about eating big juicy steaks instead of ears and tails. The squirrel became ungrateful, bitter, and crabby.

He complained to the lion about the hard work in cleaning up the den. "You're always leaving hair clumps from your mane all over the place," the squirrel whined one day. "You snore when you sleep, you stink the place up with your rotten-meat belches, and I never get enough to eat."

The lion eyed his little friend. "You don't get enough to eat?" he queried.

"No, I don't!" the little squirrel pouted. "I'm sure the reason I'm so small is because you never give me enough to eat. Why, I'll bet I could eat a whole impala if I ever got the chance."

The lion snarled in anger. "You ungrateful little squirrel! You don't appreciate all I've done for you. I'm going to put you to the test. Tomorrow I'll go and kill an impala and bring you the whole animal. You'll show me if you can eat that much meat at once. If you finish the meat, I'll apologize and give you a larger share of the meat in the future. But," the lion paused for emphasis, "if you can't eat the whole impala, then I will kill you because of your whining, complaining attitude."

The squirrel gulped. But he stared back at the lion and taunted, "Bring on the meat!"

"Tomorrow morning," the lion roared, "I'll kill an impala by the water hole and then sit and watch you eat until you pop. You're so scrawny, you'll never eat a whole impala."

"I'm only tiny because you never feed me enough!" the squirrel shot back. "Just watch how much I can eat tomorrow."

That evening as the lion slept, the squirrel sneaked out of the den and called all the other squirrels in the area. "I need your help," he said. "Everyone gather under the fallen acacia tree by the water hole tomorrow morning and I'll tell you what to do." All the other squirrels agreed to help.

The lion woke up and stretched in the dark hours before dawn the next day. Then he prowled through the curtain of blackness and crouched by the water hole. When a young impala buck skittered up to drink, the lion pounced. He dragged the dead impala away from the water hole and called the squirrel. Leading the squirrel back to the impala, the lion settled down and told him, "Go ahead and eat. And remember, if you don't eat the whole thing, that will be the end of you."

The squirrel nodded and started nibbling at the meat. He soon became full. The lion licked his velvety black lips, revealing sharp, meat-stained fangs. "Are you full already?" he asked.

The squirrel burped politely, which is the custom in Africa, and said, "All this meat is making me thirsty. I need to go to the water hole for a drink. Then I'll come back and eat some more meat."

The lion agreed. The squirrel scurried down to the fallen acacia tree by the water hole and found all the squirrels waiting for him. "The lion expects me to eat the whole impala," the squirrel explained. "But I'm already full and I've barely started. So now it's someone else's turn. Go on up to where the lion is guarding the dead impala. Eat as much meat as you can. Then tell him you're thirsty. Come down here and we'll send up the next squirrel. It will be like tag-team wrestling."

The next squirrel went up and ate. When he was full, he asked permission to get a drink, and when he reached the fallen acacia tree, he sent up the next squirrel, then the next, and the next.

The squirrel's plan worked. The lion couldn't tell the difference between the squirrels and was amazed at the amount of meat being eaten. Perhaps he had really starved his little housekeeper and began preparing an apology. Only one small scrap of meat remained when the squirrel that was eating said he needed a drink and waddled down to the water hole. They sent up the very last squirrel to finish off the meat.

The last squirrel, however, had bad eyesight and a poor memory. The others had to tell him about ten times what to do. "Finish off the meat, finish off the meat," the last squirrel repeated to himself. He squinted to see the path and set off to look for the final piece of meat. But he couldn't find it.

The lion saw this squirrel with furrowed eyebrows as he wandered back and forth muttering under his breath, "Finish off the meat, finish off the meat." The lion worried that maybe all the meat had affected the squirrel's mind and he got up to help. The squirrel sensed the movement and moved toward the lion and bumped right into the lion's leg. Then looking up into the lion's broad, whiskered face, the squirrel asked, "Oh! It's a lion. Please, mister lion, can you tell me where the impala meat is that the rest of the squirrels have been eating? I'm supposed to finish off the meat."

The lion roared in anger when he realized he'd been tricked. He bounded down to the water hole. The squirrels stopped chuckling at their wonderful trick and feared for their lives. But they'd all eaten too much, their bellies dragged, and they couldn't run for the trees. So they dug holes in the sandy soil and hid from the angry lion, which is why squirrels in Africa live in holes in the ground instead of in trees.

This fun folk tale points out the truth about the importance of giving thanks. When we forget to be thankful, we become ungrateful, complaining people which may lead to correction from God. To give thanks is to remember what God has done and is, in fact, central in maintaining a relationship with God. The opposite of remembering is forgetting. When we forget what God has done, we complain and worry and live miserable, ungrateful, selfish lives.

Israel Forgets God's Miracles

We can see this acted out in the history of Israel. Psalm 106 was written to remind the people of Israel to look back at their history and remember what God had done and to give him thanks. "Praise the LORD," the psalm begins, "Give thanks to the LORD, for he is good; his love endures forever. Who can proclaim the mighty acts of the LORD or fully declare his praise?" (vv. 1–2).

The writer begins by remembering. In fact, he asks an unanswerable question—Who can proclaim the mighty things God has done? No one can fully delve into the depth of it all. If we tried to write it, our list would go on forever. When we realize God is the Creator and Sustainer of the universe, we acknowledge that everything we have comes from his hand. Air, water, our flesh and bones, our food, our thoughts, everything comes from God.

Elihu, the wisest of Job's counselors, put it this way: "If it were his intention and he withdrew his spirit and breath, all mankind would perish" (Job 34:14–15). The list really is endless. It's impossible for us as finite beings to proclaim fully the mighty acts of the Lord. But we must give thanks as best we can or we will forget what God has done.

The writer of Psalm 106 gives a quick history of the people of Israel from their time in Egypt through their captivity in Babylon. It is a history of God's miracles to save Israel and Israel's ingratitude. Each time God did a wondrous thing for them they soon forsook him and returned to sin.

Three times the psalmist mentions something that is the key to the Israelites' struggles. In Psalm 106:7 we read, "When our fathers were in Egypt, they gave no thought to your miracles; they did not remember your many kindnesses, and they rebelled by the sea, the Red Sea." God had done great miracles in Egypt. He had shown his awesome power as he turned the Nile to blood, sent frogs and gnats to cover the country, turned the day to night, and more. He then rescued the Israelites from slavery in Egypt and led them to the Red Sea.

But Pharaoh had pursued them. His former slaves were trapped between the desert and the water. As Pharaoh approached with his army, the Israelites looked back in terror. They forgot all the miraculous things God had already done. They said to Moses, "Weren't there enough graves in Egypt? Why did you bring us to the desert to die? It would have been better to stay as slaves to the Egyptians than to die in the desert."

Even though God's miracles in Egypt should have been in their short-term memory bank, the psalmist says the people forgot what God had done and they rebelled. When we don't remember, we start turning away from God. Maybe our rebellion is subtle at first. But we begin to rely more and more upon ourselves and leave God out of the picture.

Moses told the people not to be afraid. He prayed and God opened up the Red Sea in another great miracle. They crossed over safely— Pharaoh followed and drowned. The psalmist then says in verse 12 that the people of Israel sang God's praises and believed his promises. "But," he writes in verse 13, "they soon forgot what he had done and did not wait for his counsel." They got hungry and thirsty in the desert and complained, demanding to know why Moses had brought them into the desert to die. They soon forgot God's great actions to save them at the Red Sea and they became ungrateful.

God provided both water and food in a miraculous way and the Israelites moved on to Mount Sinai. But while Moses was on the mountain with God receiving the Ten Commandments, the people of Israel made a gold idol of a calf and worshiped it. Why? Psalm 106:21 says, "They forgot the God who saved them, who had done great things in Egypt." When we forget what God has done, we become ungrateful and start whining and complaining. God is not pleased.

The rest of Psalm 106 shows the Israelites going from problem to problem, falling into sin, rebelling against God. What was the basic cause? They forgot what God had done for them in the past. They did not remember, nor did they give thanks. As they forgot God's miracles, they walked away from God and into all kinds of sin.

Near the end of Psalm 106, the Israelites have been scattered as captives in the nations as punishment for their sin. God hears their cry for help and remembers his covenant and comes to rescue them. And to emphasize his point, the writer encourages Israel to give thanks. He writes in verse 47, "Save us, O Lord our God, and gather us from the nations, that we may give thanks to your holy name and glory in your praise." When God saves us, helps us, and does something great for us, we need to give thanks to God for what he has done. But first we need to remember. Remembering what God has done is the first step in giving thanks.

Remembering is such an important part of giving thanks that when Joshua led the people of Israel into the Promised Land one generation later, God told him to build a mound of stones as a memorial. God didn't want the Israelites to forget what he'd done (Josh. 4:1–9).

A fictionalized version of that crossing of the Jordan River easily comes to mind when reading the account in Joshua 3–4.

A Heap of Stones

Elishama looked fearfully at the rushing waters of the Jordan River. He gripped his father's hand and looked up. His father rubbed the top of his head. "Don't fear, Elishama. God will go before us," he whispered. "Now listen to our leader, Joshua."

Elishama struggled to hear the voice of the white-haired old man as he stood in the middle of the people. "As soon as the priests who carry the ark of the Lord—the Lord of all the earth—set foot in the Jordan, its waters flowing downstream will be cut off and stand up in a heap."

Elishama eyed the muddy brown water from the Jordan that lapped over the edge of the riverbank. He had heard about the miracle of God blowing a path through the Red Sea when his grandparents had left Egypt. But could God really hold back the water from this river?

The priests went ahead with the ark balanced on long poles, which they carried on their shoulders. Elishama's father hoisted him atop his shoulders so that the boy could see. The priests stepped into the water and it seemed like the water shrank away from them. It stopped upstream and piled up higher and higher, while the water below ran off toward the Dead Sea. The priests stood on dry ground.

A thunderous cry filled the air as the people shouted out when they saw what had happened. God had done a miracle. The line of people started moving, keeping well downstream from the ark. Elishama's father tightly held his son's hand as they joined the jostling throng, hurrying across the river. "Did you see what happened?" Elishama asked his father. "Is it God who's holding the water back?"

Elishama and his family joined the rest of the people on the far side of the river. After everyone had crossed, the priests stood alone in the river. Then Joshua called out for twelve men who had been appointed earlier. Elishama watched as Joshua sent these men back into the dry riverbed. Each one picked up a large stone from the middle of the riverbed and balanced it on his shoulder to carry away.

"What does this mean?" Elishama asked his father. "Why are they carrying those twelve large stones?"

Before his father could answer, Elishama heard Joshua's voice, "These stones are to serve as a sign among you. In the future, when your children ask you, 'What do these stones mean?' tell them that the flow of the Jordan was cut off before the ark of the covenant of the Lord. These stones are to be a memorial to the people of Israel forever."

Soon after the men had carried the stones out of the river, the priests with the ark of the covenant came up out of the Jordan. Elishama watched as they stepped up onto the bank. As soon as the last priest stepped onto dry ground, Elishama heard the roaring of rushing water. The heap of water filled the river and it ran over its banks as before. Elishama knew he'd seen a miracle as great as when God had opened a way through the Red Sea.

Later when they moved camp to Gilgal, Elishama stood as close as he could as Joshua directed the people to set up the stones from the river. He listened as Joshua spoke again: "The Lord your God dried up the Jordan before you until you had crossed over. The Lord your God did to the Jordan just what he had done to the Red Sea when he dried it up before us until we had crossed over. He did this so that all the peoples of the earth might know that the hand of the Lord is powerful and so that you might always fear the Lord your God."

Elishama looked at the heap of twelve rocks and remembered

the water heaped up behind the priests. "Whenever I look at these rocks," he vowed, "I will remember what God did and I will thank him and tell the story to my children."

Always Give Thanks

We need personal memorial stones. We need to remember what God has done, and then we need to give thanks to God. He loves it when we give him thanks.

Paul's prayers in the letters he wrote to the early churches are drenched with thanksgiving. "We always thank God for all of you, mentioning you in our prayers," he tells them in 1 Thessalonians 1:2. "We always thank God, the Father of our Lord Jesus Christ, when we pray for you," he writes in Colossians 1:3. He gives this command in Philippians 4:6: "Do not be anxious about anything, but in everything, by prayer and petition, with thanksgiving, present your requests to God." Paul thanked God every time he remembered the Philippians, and he commanded the Thessalonians to give thanks in all circumstances.

Thanksgiving must be an integral part of our prayers whenever we pray. So how do we give thanks on a prayer day? Somewhere early in our day, before bringing any requests to God, it's good to sit back and think about what God has done and to let our minds go back to the day we were given salvation. We can think back even earlier, to times God protected us so that later we could accept his gift of salvation.

Thanks for Saving Me

When Sarababi, an old Dorobo man, looked back on his life, he started by thanking God. Sarababi, a white-haired Dorobo tracker, had a permanent limp from a close encounter with a buffalo. He smiled when I asked him to give his testimony. He had only been a Christian a few months. He stood up and thanked God for saving him from an elephant. I thought that was an odd way to start a testimony.

Years before, while tracking animals for a big game safari company, Sarababi had led an elephant hunt. Following the elephant tracks through the forest, he got ahead of the others. As he pushed aside some tall, yellow grass, he found himself face to face with a big bull elephant.

Not knowing what else to do, Sarababi dropped to the ground and pretended to be dead. The next thing he knew, he felt the elephant sliding its tusks under his body and lifting him up. He thought he would be killed, but the elephant carried him gently. Sarababi opened his eyes briefly and saw he was dangling in the air. He closed his eyes again in fear.

Then the elephant lowered him to the ground. Sarababi continued to squeeze his eyes shut. He heard a ripping sound, and when he peeked he saw the elephant pulling out large chunks of grass by the roots. The elephant dropped the grass on Sarababi and tore branches from a tree. Soon the elephant finished burying Sarababi in grass and branches and left.

Sarababi heard the other trackers and the white hunters calling for him. He felt too stunned to call out. Then one of trackers shouted that Sarababi must be dead as the elephant had buried him. They pulled the grass and branches off, and when they got down to Sarababi, he jumped up and startled all of them.

It took Sarababi several weeks to get over the shock of being carried around by that elephant. Now, years later, he told us with gleaming eyes how he'd accepted Christ as his personal Savior after we had brought the gospel message to his village. Sarababi thanked God for rescuing him from the elephant so that one day he could believe in Jesus.

We can ask God to help us remember. As we remember, we can write down everything we are thankful for, using small notebooks or prayer journals that we can refer to at a later date. These journals can become our personal memorial stones, a record of God's goodness and faithfulness to share with our families. After remembering, it's time to get on our knees and thank God. We should thank him with a heart filled with appreciation like the one healed leper who remembered to thank Jesus for his miraculous healing.

After giving thanks for the things on our list, we'll find our attitudes change, because thankfulness is an attitude, a way of living. By remembering what God has done, our outlook on life can become filled with thanks. And when we reflect on how much God has already done, we are assured he will be able to handle any needs we bring to him now.

seven

LISTENING TO GOD'S VOICE

My sheep listen to my voice; I know them, and they follow me.

—John 10:27

ONE BIG ADVANTAGE OF HAVING a personal prayer retreat is having time to listen. When planning a prayer retreat, set aside time just to listen to God speak. Listen after praising, after confessing sins and failures, after thanking God for his amazing showers of grace, or after laying burdens at his feet. Take time to listen.

We may need guidance on a specific question or point, or we may just want God to affirm his love for us. Sometime during our prayer day, we should have the attitude that was expressed in Samuel's prayer: "Speak, LORD, for your servant is listening" (1 Sam. 3:9). And then we need to listen.

Turn Off the Noise

I went to a dance during my first month in college. Having grown up in a protected Christian environment at a school for missionary kids in Kenya, I felt quite worldly attending the dance. I asked a girl to dance with me. To my surprise, she agreed. I'd never danced before, so I don't know if I moved the right way or not.

After that first dance, we sat down at a table to talk. But the band played so loudly, I couldn't hear a word the girl said. I had to shout to tell her my name. Beyond the exchange of names, the conversation stalled. The room reverberated with the sound of guitars and drums. It was just too loud for us to talk. I eventually left, my head aching from the noise.

It's impossible to talk or hold a meaningful conversation when there's too much noise. Many times we say we can't hear God speaking to us. Maybe it's because there's just too much noise, not just noise from a loud band, but the noise of everyday events. Our lives are inundated with noise: TV, radio, CD player, family members, cheering at the ball game, even sermons, and Bible study teachers. And there's the noise in our heads as we try to figure out what happens next in our clogged schedules.

David knew what it was like to be surrounded by people, noise, interruptions, and distractions. And at a deeper level he understood the chaos possible in nature and in the events of humankind. He knew the dread and anxiety that can accompany the threat of such chaos and how the potential for chaos can distract us from our dependence upon God. So in regard to both the superficial and the deeper noises that can distract us, he wrote, "Be still, and know that I am God" (Ps. 46:10). Do you want to hear from God in all those moments when our souls are troubled. Be still. Find a quiet place. Turn off the noise. Listen.

Avoid Listening to Ourselves

Listening is a skill, something that we can learn to do. As with any skill, we improve with practice. But we need to exercise spiritual discernment, taking care to avoid the danger of listening to our will and thinking it's God's voice.

I know more than a few young men in Kenya who have prayed about a wife and thought they heard God's voice telling them to marry a certain beautiful girl. So they go to the young lady with a word from the Lord that they should marry. How can a young lady say no to a clear word from the Lord?

The first way to avoid the danger of putting our will in place of God's voice is to compare the leading we seem to have from God to the Scriptures, which is how God speaks to us directly. One young man in Kenya told a girl he'd heard God's voice telling him to marry her. But he wanted to "test" her before marriage to see if she could bear children. This young lady didn't need a voice from the clouds to hear God's Word telling her to flee sexual immorality. If what we think we hear goes against the Bible, it's not the voice of God. Rather, agreement with God's Word should be accompanied by a sense of peace and joy, not by inner turmoil and sadness or fear.

Besides the Scriptures and other believers, the elements of time serves as another external test. Sometimes it's profitable to allow a time of waiting to see if God will further confirm his voice, to see if we hear his voice consistently, and to see if believers will still agree after some time has passed.

A second check is to share with other mature believers what we think God is leading us to do. A young man who believes it is God's will that he marry a certain young woman should consult his parents and other believers who know both of them. It goes without saying that he should also consult the object of his affection. If she doesn't feel the same leading from the Lord, then the couple needs to hold off before stepping into marriage. She could respond, "It's interesting that God has told you to marry me. I haven't heard anything about it."

But if the word you receive doesn't disagree with Scripture and if, after discussing it with other believers and waiting for a period of time, it seems to be the right thing to do, then go ahead and take whatever step the Lord has prompted.

Obey God's Voice

I've learned that when God speaks to me, I need to obey. As I obey, more is revealed. When I start saying to myself, "No, that's not something I'm going to do," I stop hearing anything from God. It's as if God says, "Why should I speak when you're not willing to do what I say?"

Not long ago I woke up on a Sunday morning. As I prayed, it seemed I should give fifty dollars in the church offering that morning. It was near the end of the month, and I had already tithed earlier in the month. We only had sixty dollars in our bank account, and it would be several days until we received our salary. It certainly seemed a foolish thing to do.

I discussed the matter with my wife. In our years as missionaries, we have often felt the Lord prompting us to give when we had little left in the bank. As we've obeyed and given, God has provided. It's not always in big ways, but he always provides enough for the day, much like his promise to the people of Israel in the wilderness. "Eat today's manna," God told them. "Don't save it up until tomorrow. I'll provide more tomorrow" (see Exod. 16:11–36).

Because of our history of seeing God provide, when I shared with my wife this prompting, she answered, "If God's telling you to give, then do it." So I gave fifty dollars in the offering. Was it foolish? Yes, by human standards. Did God provide for the next few days without being able to draw money from the bank? Yes, but not with a big check in the mail or an anonymous gift. But my wife did find a check for ten dollars someone had given to her to pay for some books. It had lain forgotten in her purse for two months. I found a twenty dollars traveler's check from a long-ago trip to Kenya and cashed that to put gas in the car. And we survived until our salary came in. Why did God want that fifty dollars? I don't know. I just gave it in the church offering, and I'm not sure exactly where it went. But I obeyed, and did what I thought the Lord wanted me to do.

From the world's eyes I did something foolish. But I checked it out with another believer, in this case my wife. And I knew God's Word encourages giving even when we don't have much.

Jesus watched a widow give an offering of two small coins, worth only a fraction of a penny. But Jesus commended her for her gift, saying, "She, out of her poverty, put in everything—all she had to live on" (Mark 12:44b). Paul wrote about a generous gift from the Macedonian churches, noting, "Out of the most severe trial, their overflowing joy and their extreme poverty welled up in rich generosity. For I testify that they gave as much as they were able, and even beyond their ability" (2 Cor. 8:2–3). Since I knew I wasn't going against Scripture and I had taken time to get counsel from my wife, I gave the money.

A Word of Caution

Even though it's important to listen to God's voice and obey it, I add a word of caution: maintain a healthy understanding about impressions that may be coming from the Holy Spirit. Take care not to be mistaken.

A woman in Nairobi felt God calling her to sell all she had and open up a certain business. She asked for the counsel of others, and most told her not to do it. She ignored their advice, certain she'd heard God. The result was a failed business and a ruined financial future. Did God lead her into that business to have it fail so she'd learn a lesson in dependency and not rely upon her financial resources? While that could be one good result from the experience, God probably did not lead her so she could fail. More likely, she mistook her own desire for God's voice. Often it is very hard to discern God's voice from our own will.

We need to listen. We need to compare what we hear with Scripture. We need to ask the advice of other mature believers. We need a space of time. We need to obey. And we do need to act with a certain amount of caution. We can say, "It seems I heard God telling me to do this, so I'm going to do it." This is different from a dogmatic, "God spoke to me and that's all I need to know." As we submit to what we see as God's leading and see God opening up the way, we can feel more confidence that we are following what God wants us to do.

The Dynamics of Listening

My third son, Blake, wanted to know where to attend college, so I prayed and asked God for guidance. I told him to pray as well. Both a Christian college and an academic private university had accepted him, and the two schools offered similar scholarships. Neither decision seemed to be outside of God's revealed Word.

After praying, it did seem the Lord might be leading toward the private university, where Blake could be close to grandparents. I gave that recommendation, and he went there for his freshman year. But after one semester, he was discontented with the school. Had we listened well to the Lord? Had we made a mistake? Part of his discomfort came out of a desire to find out what God wanted him to do with his life. When he'd left high school, he only wanted a college degree from a good school to get a good job and good pay. But now he felt maybe God wanted him to work in a field where he could influence young people for the Lord.

We took a morning after his first semester to pray and fast and ask the Lord to show us whether he should stay or transfer to a Christian college. We took about half an hour that morning to praise the Lord, going through several psalms. We praised God for his complete knowledge. We praised God because he is our refuge. Then we spent a time in personal confession, asking the Lord for forgiveness in various areas of our lives. A session of thanksgiving followed, where we traced God's faithfulness to our family over the past years. Then we brought our request for guidance to the Lord. We told God we didn't know exactly what steps to take. We acknowledged his lordship and asked for guidance, and then we sat quietly and listened.

After listening for about half an hour, we compared notes. Blake felt clearly that he should leave the university, but I still felt God's direction that he should stay. As I had prayed, I had argued with God. Why should he stay? It's expensive, and he's being exposed to drunkenness and immorality at an uncomfortable level in the dorm. The Lord seemed to tell me that Blake should stay so he could see the depth of sin and where it leads. Blake should finish the year, then move to another school the following fall. I didn't get a flashing neon sign in my mind telling what school that might be, only the impression that Blake should make a careful search based on his desire to work with children, perhaps as a teacher overseas.

Blake felt at peace about this course of action, but I still had second thoughts. Maybe I had manipulated the situation. It would have been possible for Blake to pull out right then and attend a community college for a semester and save a bundle on school loans. My wife felt that this would be a better option. Had I received direction? Had we made the right decision? Blake felt it was the right direction, so he finished out the second semester before transfer-ring to a Christian school.

Listening to God takes time and quietness, and continually test-ing our decisions against our doubts about whether we are follow-ing God or our own wishes. I believe that if we listen carefully and act accordingly, we can be more open and sensitive to his leading.

Jack and Gayle Taylor from Canada have been learning as a fam-ily to listen to God. They've set aside several prayer days for major decisions in their lives as well as for times of personal renewal. Sometimes they wander the woods or beaches on personal prayer days. But their most intense prayer retreat came as they struggled to decide whether they should leave Kenya after eighteen years as missionaries at Rift Valley Academy. Moving back to Canada would mean major changes in the lives of their three children, and Jack and Gayle felt their children had to help make the decision.

Health concerns during their years in Kenya had taken a toll on Jack's body. A tropical disease specialist recommended that they leave Kenya. But Jack and Gayle didn't feel ready to move away from the country that had become home to them and their three children. Their son, Richard, had just graduated from high school and the family accompanied Jack to North America. Another tropi-cal disease specialist in Canada confirmed the first diagnosis on Jack's health, and he made a similar recommendation that they should stay in Canada. Still, the Taylors weren't convinced. Then their financial support dropped off suddenly to under 50 percent. The mission required 100 percent support for a return to Kenya.

They prayed and asked God to provide support and spoke in various churches, but nothing came in. The Taylors wanted to go back. The school in Kenya expected them and desperately needed them on staff. They had prayerfully set a deadline for receiving the needed support.

On that last weekend before the deadline to make a decision, they hunkered down as a family in Jack's parent's place while his parents were away. The Taylor family began to talk and pray. Michelle and Laura had been born and raised in Kenya, while Richard, the oldest, had his first birthday on the plane heading toward Africa. Kenya had become home to everyone in the Taylor family. They hated the thought of leaving, despite what doctors or mission boards wanted. Perhaps God might yet work a miracle in answer to their prayers.

The family talked openly and expressed a lot of emotion as together they faced this time of decision. Jack and Gayle felt if God wanted to bring them home to stay in Canada, he would have to confirm this step to their children. They didn't want to see their children's faith shattered at such a crucial time in their lives. Michelle was in grade 11, Laura in grade 9, and Richard was entering his second year at Trinity Western University.

Gayle shared with Richard, Michelle, and Laura what they usually do at times when they really need to hear from God. Jack and Gayle make it a practice to walk and talk with God each morning around a park, but for special occasions they prepare for dialogue and communication.

They gave each of their kids a sheet of paper and went over it as a family. Jack and Gayle wanted their children to know they could listen to God as well. First they listed some advice on being quiet and listening to God's voice.

- Listen for God's voice—seek his direction.
- Seek silence: it brings us near to God.
- In silence, God's still small voice is heard.
- Out of silence, true peace is born in our hearts.

Jack had also written out the structure of a prayer he found very helpful in listening to his Abba's voice, especially when he had something specific to ask God or when it seemed the Lord's leading and guiding in a certain direction was unclear. Jack explained how he sometimes used this structure when he went on a spiritual retreat of a couple of hours or more, or at other times when he went out on a walk and wanted to ask God something about his life. Jack stressed how he is always very careful to make sure that what he hears lines up with Scripture. Here's the basic structure of the prayer:

Abba, Father, I come to you this morning (afternoon, evening) and pray that this room (or wherever) will be a sanctuary of your truth. Cleanse my heart and soul. As David prayed in Psalm 51, have mercy on me, O God; according to your great compassion blot out my transgressions. Wash away all my iniquity and cleanse me from my sin. Surely you desire truth in the inner parts; you teach me wisdom in the inmost place. Create in me a pure heart, O God, and renew a steadfast spirit within me. Do not cast me from your presence or take your Holy Spirit from me. Restore to me the joy of your salvation and grant me a willing spirit to sustain me (for a willing spirit makes things easy to do, it gives me joy in what is done, and the experience is not draining). The sacrifices of God are a broken spirit; a broken and contrite heart, O God, you will not despise.

I want to hear your voice and no other. So Satan (he must be rebuked out loud as Satan cannot read your thoughts), in the name of the Lord Jesus Christ and by his precious blood, I rebuke you and all your evil host. I bind you and command you to leave this place right now. Father, please rebuke the working of the Evil One with your own precious self. Send your guardian angels to protect me in this place. Set your hedge of protection around me and your umbrella of protection over me.

Come, Holy Spirit, and minister your truth in the very depths of my being. Come, Abba Father, and whisper your truth to my heart. Come, precious brother Jesus, and stand with me during this very vulnerable time. I will give you all the glory for your direction and ministry. I love you all.

Jack told his children to pray slowly through this prayer and then listen and write down their Abba's response to them. They should write down whatever God brought into their minds. Jack noted that the Lord would probably lead them to Scripture to back up what he told them.

Jack and Gayle also wrote down some meaningful verses to help them get started on this quiet time with the Lord, but they encouraged their children to go where God led them during their quiet time with him.

For example the last six verses of Psalm 73 could be prayed back to God like this:

Yet I am always with you; you hold me by my right hand. You guide me with your counsel, and afterward you will take me into glory. Whom have I in heaven but you? And earth has nothing I desire besides you. My flesh and my heart may fail, but you, God, are the strength of my heart and my portion forever. As for me, it is good to be near you. I make you, O Sovereign Lord, my refuge.

The family separated for several hours to spend time alone with the Lord to pray and listen. At the appointed time they came back. They asked each of their children, "What did God say to you?" Each of the kids had a special word from the Lord, which fit their special concerns and their personality. God had spoken with special promises and with special care to confirm in their minds that the family would be coming home to stay in Canada. But God also added a nice surprise. All the Taylors received the same direction. They should head back to Kenya for six months to say their good-byes, do their work at the school, and sell out and pack up in an orderly manner. God said he would supply for those six months. The Taylors celebrated their time with a special meal. They felt a sense of sadness at leaving Africa, but they also had joy and hope for the future because God had spoken so clearly to all of them.

Within weeks God had supplied all they needed to go back for the end of their sojourn in Africa. God even supplied enough funds to bring Jack's pastoral library home to Canada. The Taylors' families and friends in Canada encouraged them during this transition, and their missionary friends in Kenya understood why they were leaving. The confidence they had gained from God's leading at that family prayer retreat gave them the strength to keep doing the next thing. By the time the Taylors had finished their final six months in Kenya, a pastoral call had come from a church in Canada, and God's direction became clear.

God had added one more bonus by speaking to Michelle in her quiet time. He said he would work it out for her to finish off her senior year at Rift Valley Academy in Kenya with her friends. It didn't seem possible at the time, but God did work it out and she successfully finished her final year of school in Africa. She wrote back to her parents over and over, "Thank you for letting me come home to Kenya for my final year."

Jack knows that having his kids in tune with God's leading took a lot of the fear out of the changes that happened as God moved the Taylors back to Canada. Jack and Gayle continue to take time to pray and listen to God's leading, taking a personal prayer retreat at a lodge in Washington. They read and prayed and wrote and walked in the woods around the lakes and stopped to pray along the trail, asking for direction regarding the new church they pastor.

A Bird and a Verse

One way God often speaks to us is by bringing to our minds some passage from Scripture we've memorized or studied in the past. Dr. Jay Rupp from Minnesota recently went on a twenty-four-hour overnight retreat, hoping to hear from God. A particular song had been ringing in his ears for the past day, "Revive Us, Lord, Revive Us." During the night on his retreat, Jay repeated John 8:47 over and over: "He who belongs to God hears what God says."

After awakening, he spoke out loud to the Lord. "What do I really want to hear or get from you, Lord? A warm bubbly feeling? A call to return to Africa or go elsewhere?" Jay realized he wanted God to speak to him in some way, but he wasn't sure he would obey God even if he spoke. Jay wondered too how God could possibly say something to him.

That morning Jay left the topic of seeking to hear God's voice, struggling with his expectations and feeling a bit disappointed. During Jay's listening time, he hadn't heard anything he could discern as God's voice.

About an hour later, Jay had what he calls a "God Sighting," when God reveals himself in some unusual way and for a particular reason.

An English sparrow flew up and perched on the window next to Jay. Jay often sits by that window, and never before had a bird landed there. The sparrow remained on the windowsill for about ten minutes, looking around and even staring at Jay. He couldn't believe the bird didn't fly away. In spite of Jay's movements and eye contact, the bird persisted and remained close by. God spoke to Jay through the sparrow and brought to his mind Matthew 10:29–30, which says not even a sparrow will fall to the ground apart from the will of God the Father. God not only knows when sparrows fall to the ground but they also don't fall outside of his perfect will.

Jay recalled how he had preached on this passage some years

before—about how God knows and cares for small, common, and relatively valueless sparrows. If God cares that much for sparrows, how much more does he care for each of us? God understands our joys and hurts and not one of them occurs outside of the mysterious way of God. We shouldn't be afraid. We are worth more than many sparrows. Now, years after Jay preached his sparrow sermon, this sparrow landed beside him as Jay asked God to speak. It seemed God had reached out to him in a very specific way. Jay felt God speaking to him, reassuring him not only of his presence, but also his loving care with the particular struggle in Jay's life at that time.

As he watched the sparrow in the window, Jay's mind spun back to the sparrow passage in Matthew. Are not two sparrows sold for a penny? Yet not one will fall apart from the will of your Father. Jay heard God's voice. Don't be afraid. I am with you. Keep on doing my will that you are doing. I am with you.

Jay didn't receive a blazing message written in the sky to move somewhere else or change his job. But God did send a sparrow to remind him gently of a treasured portion from the Bible. Through a sparrow, God assured Jay that he cared about every aspect of Jay's life. And God's quiet voice strengthened and encouraged Jay to keep on doing what God has assigned him to do.

A Vision from God

"Are we in the wrong place?" Len and Vera Russell asked themselves—and God—soon after they came to Nairobi, Kenya, to work with a ministry to refugees. After seeing the work, they didn't feel they could cope with the needs and scope of the ministry. They had a chance to go for a short time to a mission guesthouse in Mombasa to fill in for someone on leave. While there, Len and Vera decided to set aside several evening sessions to ask God for his guidance. They prayed together and then sat quietly and listened for God's voice. After one listening session, Len asked Vera, "Have you heard anything from the Lord yet?" Vera confided that she had heard something, but she didn't want to tell him just yet.

Len then shared that he had seen a vivid picture. He'd never had a vision of anything before, but as he'd prayed and listened, he had clearly seen a tree covered with a slimy green grunge. Much scraping removed the outer coating to reveal clean shiny wood underneath. What did the vision mean? Len thought maybe it meant to get rid of the old and start anew. But he wasn't sure. Len pondered his vision and kept asking himself what they could do to make the ministry more suitable to their abilities.

Len and Vera had spent about thirty years in the United Kingdom running various businesses. They weren't teachers and wouldn't be able to teach the refugees who came to the ministry for help. At this point, the ministry had taken on 150 refugees and taught them in various craft skills so they could produce items for sale. Len felt they couldn't work with 150 at one time. So he wondered what would happen if they cut the number down to sixty. They could graduate the current refugees, having already given them several years of teaching and income-generating skills. Then they could start with sixty new refugees. They could work with these refugees for one year, teaching them as much as possible in skills such as woodworking, car mechanics, English, dressmaking, and crafts. During the year, they would have a chance to share the gospel with the refugees and disciple those who became Christians. At the end of the year, those sixty would graduate and they could take on sixty new refugees.

Len thought, *Maybe with our business skills, Vera could watch over the work and I can do the administration.* Len sat down with paper and pen and roughed out his ideas for changes at the ministry. After several mornings organizing his thoughts, he called Vera and showed her his plan and asked her what she thought. Vera read it through and then looked at Len. "Here's what God gave me the other night while we were praying and listening. It was like the Lord said, 'I will give Len a plan. Listen to him.'"

Len is thankful she didn't tell him this at the beginning. "It would have put a lot of pressure on me to come up with a plan." But God impressed on Len's heart some changes and ways to make the refugee ministry more effective.

They felt God had revealed his plan to them as they prayed and asked him for guidance. The Russells returned to Nairobi and shared their new vision for the ministry. The others involved felt the changes would work. They implemented the changes, and the refugee ministry went forward for the next six years until the Kenya government ended refugee status for those in the program. Many refugees received practical training, God's Word, and discipleship, following the plan the Lord had given to Len after he and Vera prayed and listened for God's guidance and leading.

God does speak. He speaks through his Word. He speaks in answer to prayer. He speaks as we find a quiet spot, pray humbly before him, and listen for his voice. Sometimes he gives direct guidance, but always in accordance with his revealed Word. Sometimes he gives quiet assurance and peace. At other times he guides us with discipline, revealing sin that must be confessed. Listening to God in prayer seems to be a lost art. But it's part of our walk with God that we need to reclaim.

In John 10:27, Jesus says, "My sheep listen to my voice; I know them, and they follow me," or, in the proper understanding of the Greek tense, they "keep on following me." That's what we need to do as we seek to follow Christ and listen to his voice. We need to make sure we're in tune with the Shepherd so we can keep on walking in his path. And as we keep following, we can listen and know for sure which path to take when we arrive at a fork in the road.

As we set aside time for a prayer retreat, let's not forget to take time to listen.

eight

PRAYING WHAT WE READ IN SCRIPTURE

Devote yourselves to prayer, being watchful and thankful.
—Colossians 4:2

HOW CAN I PRAY FOR A WHOLE HOUR? Several hours? A day? Sometimes it's hard to know what to pray about. Once we pray for our families, needs from our communities, and friends from church, where do we go? What do we pray about when we don't have specific information?

One good way to pray is to open the Bible and start reading. As we read, we can pray back to the Lord the things we're reading and learning. We can pray back requests for ourselves as the Spirit challenges us in certain areas where we might be falling short of God's best. Or we can pray for our pastor or friends according to what we've just read. The Epistles are filled with things we can pray back to God, even if they're not written as prayers. The Gospels give us intimate pictures of Christ's life and his teaching, which are rich with prayer subjects connected to our world.

As we read the Bible, we let the Word itself direct us in the kinds of things to pray about. If we have some people on our hearts, certain passages will spark us to think about them and we can pray what we've just read. Reading and praying Scripture is kind of a free-flowing prayer time that follows where the passage is going. I think about it as an adventure in finding and praying for God's will. Here's an example of Scripture-directed prayer.

Praying for Dorobo

We had just planted our first church among the Dorobo tribe in a mountain village called Eburru in 1994. We had been going to Eburru, making friends, learning their culture, and sharing Old Testament stories. Finally after several years we shared the gospel. The first fourteen Dorobo had believed in Jesus just weeks before. But as I prayed for this new church, I felt afraid. How could I preach the Word to the unreached Dorobo? Had these first believers really understood the decision they had made to follow Christ? How would I be able to disciple them?

As I prayed, I recalled some verses I'd been memorizing from 1 Corinthians 2:1–5: "When I came to you, brothers, I did not come with eloquence or superior wisdom as I proclaimed to you the testimony about God. For I resolved to know nothing while I was with you except Jesus Christ and him crucified. I came to you in weakness and fear, and with much trembling. My message and my preaching were not with wise and persuasive words, but with a demonstration of the Spirit's power, so that your faith might not rest on men's wisdom, but on God's power."

These verses touched me. I had felt the same weakness and fear Paul felt as I told Old Testament stories in the village for a year to build a foundation of understanding so the Dorobo could understand what Christ did at the cross. As I prayed, I turned these verses from 1 Corinthians into my prayer for the Dorobo.

I talked to the Lord, admitting my fear and trembling. I told God I didn't feel I'd done a very good job of explaining the Old Testament stories. I didn't feel I'd been eloquent. Not knowing the Maasai language that the Dorobo use, I'd been reduced to showing pictures and playing a tape with the stories narrated in Maasai. Then I'd asked questions in Swahili to see if they'd understood. It all seemed like a bumbling mess. After a year of explaining God's holiness and man's sinfulness, we had shown the Jesus film in Maasai. Now that we had our first believers, I worried that some had only believed because of the modern technology of a film.

"Lord, my message has not been eloquent, but I have been proclaiming the testimony about you, God, to this tribe." I told God I didn't think my preaching was persuasive or wise. I wanted the faith of our new believers to rest on God's power. So I prayed God would demonstrate the power of his Spirit to the Dorobo. "Show the Dorobo your power, God," I prayed, "so that their faith might not rest on my wisdom, or the technology of a film show, but on your power." I prayed those verses back to God throughout that week.

The next Sunday at Eburru, Paulina, one of the new believers, asked if we could help her sister-in-law, Susannah. Paulina said Susannah acted crazy. She would take off her clothes and run around the village naked, scaring the children and shouting nonsense. Paulina confided that Susannah had been fine when she'd left the village some years before to be married as a second wife to a man in a neighboring area. But when she came back, she was out of her mind.

I felt tingles going down my back as I listened. It had all the signs of demonic possession and I felt scared. But we'd asked the Lord to demonstrate the Spirit's power so the faith of our new Dorobo believers would rest on God's power. So I told Paulina we could pray for Susannah. "I know God can help her," I said, but inside I felt a weakness in my gut. "God, I know you're answering my prayer for you to show your power. But I don't know what to do! Help!" I prayed. I asked for a week so we could gather some prayer support.

Back at our mission station at Kijabe, we asked our prayer group to pray so Susannah could be released from the power of Satan. We had a burden and prayed through the week as we went about our normal routines. But I did not set aside a special day for prayer.

The next Sunday we took four other missionaries with us as we drove up to Eburru. We held a church service for the new Christians, then, after the service, we gathered in Paulina's house to pray for Susannah. We asked questions to determine the source of the demonic spirits, but Susannah gave us confusing answers. We talked and prayed for well over an hour, some of our team praying in their hearts, while I prayed out loud and talked with Susannah through Paulina, who translated my Swahili into Maasai. Things kept getting more and more confused. We prayed against a spirit of confusion, but nothing seemed to work.

Finally, I decided to call off our session so we could go home and pray some more. But before closing, I asked Susannah if she wanted to be free from the demons plaguing her. She said yes. I asked if she wanted to accept Christ as her Savior. She said yes. So I had Susannah pray after me and took her through a prayer of confession of sins and accepting Christ's gift of forgiveness and salvation. It seemed she just mumbled through the prayer to get us off her back. When we finished, we told Paulina we'd come back the next Sunday to pray some more.

During that week, I went back to those verses in 1 Corinthians and prayed them again. "Demonstrate your Spirit's power, Lord, so the faith of these Dorobo believers will not rest on men's wisdom, but on your power alone." The Lord convicted me I hadn't prayed enough. The Lord took me to Mark 9 and the story of the time Jesus' disciples failed to drive out the demons in a young boy. Jesus took over and commanded the deaf and mute spirit to leave. When the disciples asked Jesus why they had failed to drive out the evil spirit, Jesus replied, "This kind can come forth by nothing, but by prayer and fasting" (Mark 9:29 KJV). I knew that the fasting part of the verse didn't appear in the oldest Greek manuscripts. But I took it as a call from God to serious prayer. Our prayer team had committed to pray for Susannah the whole week, and I set Thursday aside as a day of personal prayer and fasting.

Because of commitments at the magazine where I worked as the editor, I couldn't take Thursday off as a prayer retreat. But I fasted for the day and prayed during the times I normally would have eaten. I asked God specifically to show his power to the Dorobo and to show us the source of these spirits so Susannah could be completely delivered.

That next Sunday we again took a team of four people to Eburru to pray for Susannah's deliverance. As we drove up the mountain we sang praise songs and songs of victory. When we arrived at the village, some of the men ran over to us. "What did you do last week?" they asked. "The day after you left, Susannah began wearing clothes and could talk sensibly for the first time since she came home."

I mumbled some answer about how God had worked, but I really didn't know what had happened. We held our service and then a small group gathered again to pray for Susannah's deliverance. This time as we talked, Susannah could understand and clearly told us the source of the demons.

She had been married as a second wife to a man near Enosopukia. The man's first wife was barren, and after Susannah had several children the first wife became jealous. She turned the husband against Susannah and the two went to a witch doctor and called down three curses on Susannah. Susannah began acting strangely and ran away to Naivasha town, where she lived briefly as a prostitute before her family brought her home to Eburru.

Susannah knew the names of the three curses that had been put upon her. Knowing that Satan and his demons can cling to a curse if the recipient isn't ready to forgive the ones who gave the curse, we asked Susannah if she could forgive her husband and her co-wife. We reminded her too that if she really believed in Jesus as her Savior, she had to forgive others just as the Lord had forgiven her.

Susannah nodded and said she wanted to forgive her husband and her co-wife. Once that happened, Satan had no hold left. We named the three curses and the demons that had entered with those curses. We reminded Satan and his demons that Jesus created them and that Jesus had triumphed over them at the cross. We reminded Satan that Jesus now sat at the right hand of God the Father in the heavenlies, high above all principalities and powers. Then we claimed our authority as believers in Christ who have also been seated in the heavenlies with Christ, and we commanded the demons to leave Susannah and not come back.

The demons left. The woman had been delivered as a demonstration of the Spirit's power. I stood back, marveling at God's power. God had answered as we'd prayed those verses from 1 Corinthians, showing his power to the new Dorobo Christians.

How to Pray What We Read

To explain how to pray verses back to God as we read Scripture, the following section looks at a variety of passages—Epistles, Gospels, Prophets, and historical narrative—and shows how to turn them into powerful prayers right from the Word of God..

While reading, look for commands and promises. Commands are things God intends for us to do. If we're not obeying a certain command, we can confess our failing and ask God to help us obey it. We can also pray for others to obey this command. When we see promises, we can remind God of those promises and ask him to fulfill them in our lives and in the lives of those around us.

Praying for Sons from 2 Timothy

Paul wrote the letter of 2 Timothy to his son in the faith, Timothy. Here are three verses from 2 Timothy 2:1–3: "You then, my son, be strong in the grace that is in Christ Jesus. And the things you have heard me say in the presence of many witnesses entrust to reliable men who will also be qualified to teach others. Endure hardship with us like a good soldier of Christ Jesus."

As I read these verses, I see three commands:

1. Timothy is told to be strong;
2. He's told to entrust the things he's heard to reliable men who can teach others;
3. He's told to endure hardship.

Based on these commands, I turn these verses into a prayer for my own sons:

> O Lord, I pray that my sons would be strong in the grace of Jesus Christ. May they understand how their salvation in you is based upon your grace alone. It is your free gift. May they stand strong in that grace, Lord. May they remember the things I have taught them about following you, Lord. And I pray they would pass on their faith and belief in you to others, who can teach others as well. I pray they would endure hardship with an attitude that honors you, Lord. I know that through hardship their faith will be strengthened and grow. May they understand that we are in a war with the Evil One. May they stand strong and endure and fight as warriors in the battle for the souls of men.

I might then read verse 4. Although it doesn't contain a command or promise, it gives the picture of a soldier wanting to please his commander. From it, I can pray that my boys desire to please God with their lives just as a soldier tries to please the commanding officer.

Verse 5 speaks of athletes competing for the prize. All my sons played sports, and I might think about the hours of practice they put in. Then I'd think about Paul's analogy between athletic events and spiritual life. I would pray that my sons would compete according to God's rules and train and strain for victory in the spiritual world as hard as they practiced and played for victory on the rugby field.

In my daily prayer time, I might stop praying at this point. But during a prayer retreat when I have more time, I can go on and read the following verses and pray them back to God. I might continue praying new things for my sons, or I might pray for someone else as I move through the text. Or I might go back over those first verses and pray them over again for someone else that God brings to my mind. The important thing is to use the Word to direct the requests we bring to God.

Praying to Sit at Jesus' Feet

Mary sat at the Lord's feet while her sister Martha hustled and hassled with getting a meal for Jesus and his disciples (Luke 10:38–42). Martha came in to chide her sister for ignoring her duties of hospitality. Jesus responded, "Martha, Martha, . . . you are worried and upset about many things, but only one thing is needed. Mary has chosen what is better, and it will not be taken away from her" (vv. 41–42).

After reading this story, we stop and think. What is the one thing that is needed? What had Mary chosen to do? Mary sat at Jesus' feet, listening. That's the one thing that is needed. How many times are we worried and upset by many things? We keep running, taking care of business, harried and upset that we're carrying so much of the load. We can stop and pray, "Lord, I'm so much like Martha. I'm so caught up in the day-to-day needs of life. Forgive me and give me a spirit to stop and sit at your feet and listen to your voice."

We could pray and thank the Lord for prompting us to take time to sit at his feet. We could plan a prayer retreat for that very purpose. We could focus our prayer outward toward some busy friends, maybe overburdened ministry leaders. We could pray that they would learn to quiet themselves and sit at Jesus' feet like Mary, and learn from him.

Seeing God's Heart from Isaiah

Isaiah wrote the Song of the Vineyard in Isaiah 5:1–7. He shows God clearing the hillside to plant his vineyard. He plucks out the stones and plants the soil with choice vines. He builds a watchtower to protect the vineyard and puts in a winepress, expecting to make grape juice from the crop. But the vineyard yielded only bad fruit.

Can you feel God's disappointment? After all his work, his care, and his nurture, the harvest is spoiled. The vineyard, as we read a few verses further on, is the house of Israel. God loved Israel, carefully planting her on the most fertile soil. He cared for her. Yet Israel yielded only bad fruit.

In these verses, we see his pain, his love for Israel, and his desire that Israel love him in return. The God of the universe bends down to check his vines for good grapes. He looks for the fruits of righteousness in the lives of his beloved nation, Israel. He wants them to be the garden of his delight. But after all he has done for his people, God only sees sin and bloodshed. The song goes on to show God destroying the vineyard, breaking down the wall, trampling on the vines, and commanding the clouds not to rain on it.

After reading this Song of the Vineyard, we should take time to digest the picture of God agonizing over his failed vineyard. We could pray, "O Lord, how discouraged you must feel when you give so much and your creation spurns you and rebels against you." Then we could put ourselves in the place of Israel and ask, "Am I a fruitful vineyard? Am I allowing the Spirit of Jesus Christ to produce the fruits of righteousness in my life? Or am I barren and in danger of destruction at the hand of the Vineyard-Wrecker?" This might lead to a time of confession: "Lord, forgive me for refusing to obey you. My life is barren. Forgive me for the times I denied you, for the times I didn't pass on grace and love to my friends." Then we could go on and pray, "Lord, let my life bear fruit. May my life be filled with the fruit of righteousness that comes through Jesus Christ."

Passages like the Song of the Vineyard aren't meant to be read quickly and dissected for something to pray, before hurrying on to the next verses. They are to be read slowly, to be tasted and their savor enjoyed. The prayers we breathe as we read these verses should come from the depths of our soul as we begin to understand God's very heart.

Praying Promises from Joshua

Recently my wife, Kym, studied and prayed through the book of Joshua. What follows are some things she learned and prayed from Joshua 1.

On her first reading, she underlined all the verses about God. Four times God speaks of giving the land to Israel. God promises to be with Joshua wherever he goes, and he also promises never to fail or forsake Joshua.

After underlining these verses about God, Kym stopped and read through them again. She gained a picture of God giving the land as an inheritance to Israel. Then she thought of how God gives us our inheritance. Thinking about inheritance reminded Kym of Ephesians. She turned to Ephesians and read in the first chapter how we as believers have obtained our inheritance in Christ. Kym spent some time praising God for the inheritance he's given us and who we are in Christ. After this time of praise and thanks, Kym confessed how little she thought about God's inheritance. She asked God to forgive her for being unappreciative.

Kym went through Joshua 1 again, this time underlining all the commands of God. God told Joshua to cross the Jordan, to be strong and courageous (three times, followed by the same message for the people), to obey the Law, not to turn away from the Law, to meditate on the Law, and to do all that is written in it. Kym asked God to enable her to be strong, to keep his commands, and to meditate on the Word.

Then Kym read the chapter again, this time underlining the promises. God promised the land, saying that no one would be able to stand against Israel. God promised to be with them and not to fail them. He promised Joshua success wherever he went, the last promise being contingent upon Joshua's fidelity in following the Law.

These promises were made to Joshua, but their principles reach through the centuries to us. Kym then spent some time asking God to share these promises with her and give her the strength to obey the commands he gave to Joshua. She tied the dependent promises to the commands, praying like this: "Lord, you promised Joshua success if he was strong and courageous and if he was careful to do the law and not to turn from it in any direction. Help me, Father, to be strong and courageous. Help me to obey your commands to live a holy life. Lord, as I grow in these graces, grant to me your presence and true success to defeat your enemies in my life."

When she completed reading and praying through Joshua 1, Kym chose verse 8 to be her prayer through the next few days: "Do not let this Book of the Law depart from your mouth; meditate on it day and night, so that you may be careful to do everything written in it. Then you will be prosperous and successful." Kym read the verse several times until she had the gist of it, so she could make it her prayer for the next few days, until she went on to pray through the next chapter of Joshua.

Pray the Word Back to the Word-Giver

These four examples from the Epistles, the Gospels, the prophecy of Isaiah, and the historical narrative of Joshua are meant to crack open the door on a new way to pray. The Bible brims with passages we can read and pray back to God. Some verses have commands, while others have promises that might be applied to our lives. Stories of God's faithfulness teach us to trust him. Other passages teach us how to live and honor God with our bodies.

Anytime we are not sure how to pray, the Word will show us. And as we read a particular book in our daily devotions, we can start with praying through that section. Read slowly. Savor the stories, the teaching, and the words. Then pray back to the Lord the things he shows to you from the Scripture.

nine

PATTERNING OUR
PRAYERS AFTER JESUS

But Jesus often withdrew to lonely places and prayed.

—Luke 5:16

JESUS STAYED IN TOUCH WITH HIS Father. Even as the crowds pressed in on him, grasping for his healing touch and listening to his teaching, Jesus knew he needed to be alone with God the Father. So he withdrew. He went to lonely places and prayed.

If we want to meet God alone and pray—for several hours, for half a day, for a full day, for a weekend—Jesus is our supreme example. The Gospels assume that when he pulled aside, he prayed all the time. We don't know all that Jesus prayed; he went alone. But we do find samples of his prayers in the Gospels. These prayers can give us direction about what kinds of things to pray for during prayer retreats. We can make the praises and requests of Jesus ours as well.

The longest recorded prayer of Jesus is found in John 17, as Jesus prayed for his disciples after they had eaten the last supper together. He prayed for himself, for his inner group of disciples, and then he

121

prayed for us—all the other believers who would follow the Way as the gospel spread around the world.

"Glorify Your Son"

Jesus had only one request for himself, but it was so vital that he prayed for it twice (John 17:1–5, 24). He asked that God the Father glorify his Son. Then at the end of the prayer he asks that those who have been saved through the cross will see him in his glory in oneness with the Father. So even as Jesus asked to be glorified by the Father, he was asking that God's name would be praised, lifted up, and honored.

Jesus said this glory would come as he completed the work the Father gave him. This was the work of dying on the cross to pay the penalty for sin so those who believed could have eternal life. As Christ completed this work, he knew it would bring glory and honor to God because men and women—condemned to die because of sin—could come to God for forgiveness and eternal life. God did answer this prayer. He did glorify the Son. Even as Jesus was lifted up on a despised cross, his death brought salvation to all those who believed. And when God's power raised Jesus from the dead, God did glorify Jesus, seating him once again at the Father's right hand in heaven.

Ultimately, all our prayers should be for God's glory. I don't often pray for God to be glorified, but God's glory is the main purpose of creation. God made the world to bring glory to himself. Thus, there's nothing more important than praying for God's glory, and we can pray for his glory in any situation. If we pray for healing, the purpose is so God can get the glory. If we pray for someone to believe in Jesus as Savior, the purpose is so God can be glorified by the lips of this new believer.

"Protect My Disciples; Make Them One"

As Jesus prayed for his twelve disciples, he knew the intense pressure they would face in the hours ahead, especially as Jesus would stumble toward Golgotha, knees buckling under the weight of his cross. Jesus knew that Satan would penetrate into the very core of his disciples' hearts with doubt and despair. He knew their tendency would be to scatter to save their own lives.

So Jesus asked God to protect the disciples. "Holy Father, protect them by the power of your name" (John 17:11). Jesus invoked the mighty, powerful name of God and asked him to protect the weak, scared disciples. Jesus explains why he asks for their protection: "so that they may be one as we are one" (v. 11), that the unity of the Trinity may be demonstrated in the lives of his followers.

In verse 15, Jesus prays again for the protection of the believers: "My prayer is not that you take them out of the world but that you protect them from the evil one." The disciples needed protection from the Evil One, who is on the attack, sometimes subtly and sometimes openly like a roaring lion. And Jesus prays, "Father protect my followers."

Jesus has one more request for his disciples in verse 17: "Sanctify them by the truth; your word is truth." Thus, Jesus prays that his followers would be set apart by the truth of God's Word.

From this prayer we gain two more very important prayer weapons for our arsenal. Following Jesus' example, we can pray for God to protect us and other believers from the Evil One so that we can be one as Jesus and God are one. And we can pray for God to sanctify us or set us apart by our understanding and obeying the truth of the Bible.

"Let My Followers Be United"

Jesus directed toward us the last part of his prayer around the table. He said, "I pray also for those who will believe in me through their message" (John 17:20). What's Jesus' request? "That all of them may be one, Father, just as you are in me and I am in you. May they also be in us so that the world may believe that you have sent me" (v. 21).

Then Jesus returns to his theme of glory. He said he's given us the glory he received from God so that we might be one as Jesus and God are one. As we believe, we receive the glory of Christ. I don't understand this mystery—Jesus' saying we have his glory in us because God the Father glorified him, and when we believe, Jesus with his glory dwells in us. Just as the glory of the Lord filled the tabernacle and the temple, we, as God's temple, are filled with Jesus and the very glory of God. Jesus said, "I in them and you in me" (v. 23). Through Christ himself, we should be filled with the glory of God so we can display the love and unity of God.

Jesus next requests something for us: "May they be brought to complete unity to let the world know that you sent me and have loved them even as you have loved me" (v. 23). Jesus prayed for unity among his followers, it being a key point in proclaiming the love of God and salvation to the world. The world is meant to look at us, the church of Christ, his very body, and see such unity that it displays and reflects the glory and oneness of the Trinity. Our unity should point others to the love of God so they might be drawn to the Father. It would seem to me that we, as a church, are often a very poor reflection of God's unity. If unity was so important to Jesus, we should pray for that same unity today.

In the next verse Jesus says that he wants us to be with him in heaven so we can see his glory—the glory the Father has given Jesus because he loved him from before the creation of the world. The unity and glory of Jesus is eternal.

From Jesus' prayer in John 17, we can emphasize a few central themes as we take time aside to pray. We can pray for God to be glorified. We can pray for protection from the Evil One. We can pray for believers to be sanctified by the truth. And we can pray that all believers would be one, just as Jesus and God are one.

I admit that these aren't my everyday requests. I have on occasion prayed for unity when there has been a divisive issue. But I'm learning to use Jesus' prayer to direct my own requests as I pray.

May They See Your Glory

A few years ago I prayed for my father, who was losing his memory to Alzheimer's. As I prayed, I felt an overwhelming urge to pray that my father would behold God's glory. Even in his confused state, I knew that my father loved the Lord. I'd been with him a year or so earlier to visit a family friend, Stan Anderson, in a nursing home. Both my dad and Stan had a hard time keeping everyday facts and events in order. But as we sat beside Stan's bed, my dad suggested they pray. I felt transported into God's presence as Stan and then my dad prayed. Their souls, still in tune with their beloved Savior, poured out in passionate prayer. I sensed God's glory in that room.

But when dad was moved into an Alzheimer's care facility, I lived in Africa, half a world away. And as I prayed, I felt moved to pray that Dad would behold God's glory. I remembered that special time of prayer in the nursing home, and I wanted my dad to be able to pray and comprehend God's glory. I hoped that even in Dad's confused state, he would still have times when his mind cleared as he prayed and could behold God's glory. A few months later my father passed away. Although I miss him, I have a real sense of peace that he is indeed beholding God's glory today in heaven.

The Lord's Prayer

Jesus didn't always pray in lonely places. One day as he prayed in a certain place, his disciples watched him. When Jesus finished praying, one of the disciples said, "Lord, teach us to pray, just as John taught his disciples" (Luke 11:1). They saw Jesus at prayer, and they wanted to be able to pray like him. Jesus gave to them what we call the "Lord's prayer."

The prayer is recorded in Luke 11:2–4 and in a slightly expanded version in Matthew 6:9–13. This prayer is valuable because it contains the basic structure that any prayer should follow. We should memorize and repeat this prayer, but we should be careful that it does not become vain repetition.

I've heard this prayer rattled off in a variety of African languages every Sunday in church at the end of the second prayer. Sometimes the prayer is said so fast that the last few lines blur together, until it is punctuated with a staccato amen at the end. Because it is so familiar, we sometimes don't even think about what we're praying, and we forget how powerful this prayer is.

The Lord's prayer gives us basic requests and themes we can use to shape all our prayer. And when we plan a personal prayer day, we can build this powerful prayer into our devotional time with God.

Here's the text of the Lord's Prayer from Matthew 6:9–13: "Our Father in heaven, hallowed be your name, your kingdom come, your will be done on earth as it is in heaven. Give us today our daily bread. Forgive us our debts, as we also have forgiven our debtors. And lead us not into temptation, but deliver us from the evil one."

"Our Father in Heaven"

God is our Father. We can come to him as a child to a loving dad. He is Abba. But he's also in heaven. He is exalted, and he is powerful. He rules the universe, yet he allows us to call him Father.

Calling God our Father wasn't part of the way people prayed before Jesus came. People had to use a priest to go to God on their behalf. The very name of the Lord, *YHWH*, I am who I am, was couched in reverence and not uttered for fear of the almighty God. Yet Jesus said we should call this awesome God our Father in heaven. Then Jesus created a way for us to have a close relationship with God.

When Jesus died on the cross, the curtain that separated men from God's holy presence was torn. Through Jesus, says Hebrews 10:11–23, we can approach the very throne room of God. He is our Father (see Rom. 8:15–17), and he wants us to come to him as his children. We are the very sons and daughters of God. When we pray, we should come with a humble attitude as children before our Father.

"Hallowed Be Your Name"

Even though we can now call God our Father because of Christ, Jesus still points out that God's name is holy. It is set apart, unknowable. God's name is very special and in many ways, although he's revealed himself to us through Jesus and through the Word of God, God is infinitely beyond our knowing. As we come before the Lord to pray, we should come quietly and reverently before the very throne of the King of the universe. And we should acknowledge that his name is holy.

"Your Kingdom Come"

The first request Jesus tells us to pray for is for God's kingdom to come. As we look at the world around us, tied up and squirming in sin and filth, we need to plead with God for his kingdom to come. We need to pray for Christ's return when he will establish his kingdom on earth. And we need to pray that we would do our part in spreading the good news of the kingdom of God so people from every tribe and nation will be ready to welcome Jesus the king when he comes to rule the earth. This kingdom attitude is often lacking from my prayers.

"Your Will Be Done"

God does have a plan for this world, and he is bringing it to completion. God's will is presently done in heaven. When God speaks, his servants, the angels, obey. Jesus said we should pray that God's will would be done on earth in the same way. We don't always understand what God's will is in a certain situation, but God knows. And praying for God's will to be done here on earth is a key part of effective praying.

When Jesus prayed in the garden of Gethsemane on the night he was betrayed, he agonized in prayer and pleaded with God to "remove this cup" from him. The cup referred to his death on the cross. Jesus knew God's will in this matter, yet as he prayed he asked God to find another way to provide salvation to the world. But he submitted himself saying, "Yet not my will, but yours be done."

This is a healthy way to pray, acknowledging that God has a divine plan. We try to discern God's will in what we pray for. But we humbly admit that we might have inserted our desire and will in place of God's, so we end by asking God to do his will, not ours. God will answer that kind of prayer according to his will.

"Give Us Our Daily Bread"

We do have physical needs. There is nothing wrong with asking God to provide our daily bread, our food, our housing, and our clothing. God knows we need these things. We shouldn't be afraid to bring even the smallest need before our Father. He is happy to hear us and to answer us.

I pray that this book will make readers more kingdom-minded in prayer. But there is nothing wrong with asking God to provide for our needs. Jesus says we should pray for our daily bread, and often God provides just enough for the day. He wants us to keep relying upon him.

We often want enough manna for the whole winter season. God told Israel to go out each morning and collect enough for the day. Anything collected beyond that would be rotten by the next day, because God wants his children to have a daily dependence upon him.

"Forgive Us"

Confession is an essential part of any time of prayer. Jesus said, "Forgive us our sins." We slip. We fall down. We can't be cleaned if we cover it up. We need to confess our sins and ask God to forgive us. He's ready and willing. "If we confess our sins, he is faithful and just and will forgive us our sins and purify us from all unrighteousness" (1 John 1:9). Jesus is careful to point out that, as we're forgiven, we need to pass that forgiveness on to others who hurt us. In fact, Jesus said that if we don't forgive others, God won't forgive us (Matt. 6:12b, 14–15; 18:21–35; Mark 11:25; Luke 6:37; 11:4). Forgiveness needs to be received in community and passed on. We all sin. God wants us to come to him regularly for forgiveness, which we can pass on to others.

"Deliver Us"

"Lead us not into temptation," Jesus told us to pray. Temptation is the step before sin. It's the place where we are tested. It's also a place where we often slip and fall. So we need to pray and ask God to keep us from temptation.

Satan is the one who tempts us, so the next phrase is key: "But deliver us from the evil one." Ask God to keep us from temptation in the first place, but when we do face temptation, pray that we will be delivered.

We saw Jesus praying for the protection of his disciples in his prayer from John 17. And before Jesus went to pray on the Mount of Olives, before being handed over to the Jews for his execution, Jesus told his disciples twice to pray that they would not fall into temptation (Luke 22:40, 46). We need to pray that God will not lead us into temptation, and we need to ask him to deliver us from the Evil One.

Jesus gave this prayer to guide us. We can compare the way we normally pray with this pattern and see whether we are praising our Father's Holy name, praying for his kingdom to come, pleading for his will to be done, asking for our daily bread, claiming forgiveness for sins, and praying that we won't be led into temptation, but delivered from the Evil One. Or we can pray through the Lord's prayer, pausing after each phrase to personalize the requests and go deeper into the different facets of the Lord's prayer. We should use this prayer as our pattern whenever we pray, not just on the day we set aside to meet with God.

ten

LEARNING TO PRAY LIKE PAUL

And pray in the Spirit on all occasions with all kinds of prayers and requests. With this in mind, be alert and always keep on praying for all the saints.

—Ephesians 6:18

IF WE'RE NOT SURE EXACTLY WHAT to pray for during a prayer retreat, a good place to start is by reading through Paul's prayers. We can lift out some of his requests for his friends and churches, and pray for those things as we bring our needs before the Lord.

A few years ago, as I prayed for my ninth-grade son, Reid, I decided to follow Paul's prayer for the believers in the church at Colosse. Using Colossians 1:11 as the basis for my prayer, I asked the Lord for my son to "be strengthened with all power according to God's glorious might so that Reid may have great endurance and patience."

I had been memorizing the book of Colossians as part of my personal devotional time, and Paul's prayer for the Colossian church in verses 9–14 struck me as a potent way to pray for my family and the Kenyan church leaders and my coworkers. Here's the whole prayer:

> For this reason, since the day we heard about you, we have not stopped praying for you and asking God to fill you with the knowledge of his will through all spiritual wisdom and understanding. And we pray this in order that you may live a life worthy of the Lord and may please him in every way: bearing fruit in every good work, growing in the knowledge of God, being strengthened with all power according to his glorious might so that you may have great endurance and patience, and joyfully giving thanks to the Father, who has qualified you to share in the inheritance of the saints in the kingdom of light. For he has rescued us from the dominion of darkness and brought us into the kingdom of the Son he loves, in whom we have redemption, the forgiveness of sins.

Praying Paul's Colossian Prayer

I incorporated Paul's requests from this prayer into my own prayer time. Since I had the verses memorized, I could pray them as I ran my early morning three-mile course through the forested ravines below the mission station where we worked in Kenya. I would pray that my coworkers would be filled with the knowledge of God's will through all spiritual wisdom and understanding. I prayed that our church leaders might live a life worthy of the Lord and please him in every way, bearing fruit in every good work, growing in the knowledge of God. I prayed the verses for my wife and family.

A Prayer for Endurance

But I prayed especially hard for my son Reid to be strengthened with all power according to God's glorious might, so that he might have great endurance and patience. I sensed Reid needed an extra amount of God's strength, power, and might so that he could endure both physically and spiritually.

When we had climbed Mount Kenya together in the middle of Reid's seventh-grade year, he had displayed a lack of plain physical endurance. At the vertical bog, when he stepped knee-deep into a slimy mud hole, he'd been ready to kick off his boots and quit. The last night, as we hiked up the scree above Mackinder's Camp, he sat down often and refused to budge.

Gently and firmly I urged him on, pointing out a nearby rock and challenging him to go five steps further and sit on that rock before he made the decision to quit. Step by step he made it to Point Lenana. And we used that mountain climbing experience as an object lesson when he got discouraged over a project at school or something else. He was learning endurance and patience. So, when I saw these verses, I decided to make them my special prayer for Reid. I prayed this prayer for well over a year.

During his ninth-grade year, we lived in the United States. I prayed this verse as I saw him endure a difficult year, longing to go home to Africa. Then, when we returned to Kenya at the beginning of his tenth-grade year, God answered the prayer in a way we didn't expect. Reid tried out for the soccer team, fully expecting to gain a place on the junior varsity. But within two days he'd been cut. He was devastated.

I comforted him through his tears. I encouraged him that he could always play basketball the next term, rugby the term after that, and try out for soccer in his junior year. Through his hurt and tears, he became determined. He ran, even though he wasn't on any team. He helped coach a team of elementary school students so he wouldn't lose his love of soccer. He decided to try out for basketball the next term. To his dismay, he got cut again. I tried to encourage him. I even told him I might have been at fault because I'd been praying for this verse from Colossians so he would learn to have endurance.

I'd forgotten that James writes that perseverance and endurance come through testing (1:2–4), and it seemed God was testing Reid's endurance. Reid didn't like hearing that, but he kept running, tried out for rugby during the third term and made the junior varsity. He worked hard on his fitness and toughness, and by his junior year, he made the junior varsity soccer team. During his senior year, he was a solid defender on the varsity soccer team.

I won't credit my prayer with Reid's ability to endure. But I do know it played a part in teaching him to stand tough and endure hard times. God used those times to strengthen him physically and spiritually. I would never have prayed on my own for those difficult experiences to come into Reid's life. But as I followed Paul's prayer and prayed for Reid to experience growth in his character, specifically for endurance, God put him through tough years and taught him endurance.

Praying for Eternal Values

Paul's prayers seem to focus more on eternal values than the prayers we often offer up to God. "Give our friends a safe trip," we pray. "Heal my cousin's broken leg." "Help the missionaries in Africa." "Bless the pastor in his work." Often our requests are not specific and seem to call on God to spare us any pain and discomfort in this life.

Don't get me wrong. God does care about our safety. Paul does pray for protection from wicked and evil men. Jesus taught us to pray, "Deliver us from the evil one," and he taught us to ask for our daily bread. But our prayers could be so much deeper. When we look at how Paul prays, we see him zooming in on requests that will help people to grow more like Christ, to know God's unfathomable love, that his good and perfect will be made manifest in every painful and difficult situation, to be counted worthy of God's calling, and to produce good works. Paul prayed for things of eternal value.

In all of our praying, but especially as we take extended time to pray, we can benefit by looking at Paul's prayers, and then use his requests as patterns for our own prayer requests as we humbly come before our Father to pray.

From one of Paul's prayers for the Thessalonian church we can lift out Paul's requests and use them as we pray. Paul wrote in 2 Thessalonians 3:5, "May the Lord direct your hearts into God's love and Christ's perseverance." Paul has a number of these mini prayers thrown into this short book.

I recently heard that some of my missionary colleagues were going through a tough time. I had just started memorizing 2 Thessalonians 3, and as I prayed for my friends, God impressed it upon my heart to pray these two requests. I asked the Lord to direct their hearts into God's love. I prayed that the troubles they were going through wouldn't distract them from the Lord, but instead direct them to God's love out of dependence. I asked God to show his love for them and to make his love evident to them.

Then, as I prayed, I pictured Christ enduring the Cross for us. He stuck it out. He stayed with the task to the bitter end. What an example of enduring (see Heb. 12:3). I asked the Lord to help my friends to have the same endurance that Christ displayed on the cross so they could bring the gospel to those who needed to hear it.

This is a simple prayer, having only two requests. But as I prayed for my friends, it helped lift my prayer above the mundane "help them in their troubles" type of prayer that I usually offer up, and instead focused on their need to see God's love and to have Christ's perseverance.

On a personal day of prayer, we can use Paul's prayers as a pattern. But we must be careful that following patterns does not become the "vain repetitions" Jesus spoke of (Matt. 6:7 KJV). If you feel you are just repeating the same thing over and over without thinking, then move on and look at another one of Paul's prayers. Draw some requests out of that prayer and start praying for the next person God puts on your heart.

Paul's Prayers

Here's a list of the prayers Paul prayed for his friends and churches as well as the prayer requests he gave to others to direct their prayers for him. All the prayers and requests come from letters he wrote to the churches he'd planted and to people involved in those churches. Each prayer is followed by a short comment and some requests pulled from the text that we can use as we pray for our loved ones, leaders, and friends during our day of prayer. And we shouldn't forget to pray some of these prayers for ourselves as well.

> I pray that now at last by God's will the way may be opened
> for me to come to you. (Rom. 1:10b)

We can pray for time with other believers to encourage them and have fellowship together.

> Brothers, my heart's desire and prayer to God for the Israel-
> ites is that they may be saved. (Rom. 10:1)

We can pray for those who don't yet know Christ that they can understand and be saved.

> Oh, the depth of the riches of the wisdom and knowledge of God! How unsearchable his judgments, and his paths beyond tracing out! "Who has known the mind of the Lord? Or who has been his counselor? Who has ever given to God, that God should repay him?" For from him and through him and to him are all things. To him be the glory forever! Amen. (Rom. 11:33–36)

This prayer is filled with praise. We can praise God for the depth of his wisdom and knowledge, his unsearchable judgments, and untraceable paths. We can praise the Lord that his mind is so great that we can never understand it and that no one needs to give God advice. We can praise God that everything comes from him and belongs to him. Then we can pray that the lives of the ones we're praying for may bring glory to God.

> Pray that I may be rescued from the unbelievers in Judea and that my service in Jerusalem may be acceptable to the saints there, so that by God's will I may come to you with joy and together with you be refreshed. The God of peace be with you all. Amen. (Rom. 15:31–33)

We can pray for the safety and rescue of those in dangerous circumstances. We can pray that we have a chance to meet with these believers and be refreshed by our time together. We can pray that God will show us ways to serve those other believers. And we can pray that God might bring his inner peace to the ones we're praying for.

Now to him who is able to establish you by my gospel and
the proclamation of Jesus Christ, according to the revelation of the mystery hidden for long ages past, but now revealed and made known through the prophetic writings by
the command of the eternal God, so that all nations might
believe and obey him—to the only wise God be glory forever through Jesus Christ! Amen. (Rom. 16:25–27)

This benediction oozes with praise to God. We can praise God for
his ability to establish believers in their faith after hearing the gospel.
Then we can pray and ask God to establish these believers. We can
praise God that the gospel has been revealed, and then we can ask
God that all nations (Greek *ethnē*, "tribes") might believe in Christ
and obey him. We can also pray that God would receive the glory
for all he is doing in the church and in the lives of our friends and
family.

Praise be to the God and Father of our Lord Jesus Christ,
the Father of compassion and the God of all comfort, who
comforts us in all our troubles, so that we can comfort those
in any trouble with the comfort we ourselves have received
from God. (2 Cor. 1:3–4)

We can praise God that he is the Father of compassion and the
God of all comfort, and then pray that God will comfort the ones
we're praying for in their troubles so they can pass that comfort on
to others who are troubled.

Three times I pleaded with the Lord to take it away from
me. (2 Cor. 12:8)

Here Paul is praying for his physical ailment, his thorn in the flesh, to be removed. We can certainly pray for physical healing as we take time to pray for the needs of those around us. We should note that even though God used Paul to heal others in miraculous ways, this is one time when God said no to Paul's request, so that in his physical weakness he would learn to depend on God alone. Even as we pray for God to bring healing, we can also pray that in their pain and physical weakness the hurting ones may learn to depend upon God, and that God's will be made manifest in their painful situation.

> Now we pray to God that you will not do anything wrong. (2 Cor. 13:7a)

We can simply ask the Lord that the people we're praying for won't do anything wrong. That includes praying that they'd understand what is right and how God wants us to act, and then for the strength to do the right thing.

> Our prayer is for your perfection. (2 Cor. 13:9b)

As Paul asks for the perfection of the Corinthian believers, he is asking that they would be mature. As long as we live in our bodies, we won't be perfect and without sin. But we can pray for people to be mature believers.

> Praise be to the God and Father of our Lord Jesus Christ, who has blessed us in the heavenly realms with every spiritual blessing in Christ. (Eph. 1:3)

Praise God that in Christ he has blessed us and those we're burdened for with all the spiritual blessings we need in Christ!

I have not stopped giving thanks for you, remembering you
in my prayers. I keep asking that the God of our Lord Jesus
Christ, the glorious Father, may give you the Spirit of wisdom and revelation, so that you may know him better. I pray
also that the eyes of your heart may be enlightened in order
that you may know the hope to which he has called you, the
riches of his glorious inheritance in the saints, and his incomparably great power for us who believe. (Eph. 1:16–19a)

As we start our prayer, we can give thanks for what God has done
in the life of the person we're praying for. Then we can ask God to
give this person the Spirit of wisdom and revelation so they can
know God even better. We can pray that they would know the
hope of our future glorious inheritance when the Lord returns,
and understand the awesome and great power that God gives to
them to live in victory now. We can pray the same request for
ourselves so we can know God better.

For this reason I kneel before the Father, from whom his
whole family in heaven and on earth derives its name. I
pray that out of his glorious riches he may strengthen you
with power through his Spirit in your inner being, so that
Christ may dwell in your hearts through faith. And I pray
that you, being rooted and established in love, may have
power, together with all the saints, to grasp how wide and
long and high and deep is the love of Christ, and to know
this love that surpasses knowledge—that you may be filled
to the measure of all the fullness of God. Now to him who
is able to do immeasurably more than all we ask or imag-
ine, according to his power that is at work within us, to
him be glory in the church and in Christ Jesus throughout
all generations, for ever and ever! Amen. (Eph. 3:14–21)

Wow, what a prayer! If God answered that prayer in our lives, it would certainly blast us into a different level of Christian living. As we fall to our knees, we could cry out, "Strengthen me, Father. May your Spirit's power flood my inner being. May my faith be big enough to allow Christ to dwell in my heart. Grant me the power to understand the love of God that is so high, so wide, so long, and so deep that it surpasses human understanding. Fill me, God, with all of your fullness. May you be glorified, almighty God. You possess the power to answer this prayer in ways that are impossible to measure by human standards." As we pray this prayer for ourselves and others, it will revolutionize lives.

> Pray also for me, that whenever I open my mouth, words may be given me so that I will fearlessly make known the mystery of the gospel, for which I am an ambassador in chains. Pray that I may declare it fearlessly, as I should. (Eph. 6:19–20)

We can pray for our missionary friends to be fearless as they declare salvation by God's grace. We can ask God to fill our mouths whenever we speak so that we too can fearlessly make known the good news of Jesus Christ.

> I thank my God every time I remember you. In all my prayers for all of you, I always pray with joy. . . . And this is my prayer: that your love may abound more and more in knowledge and depth of insight, so that you may be able to discern what is best and may be pure and blameless until the day of Christ, filled with the fruit of righteousness that comes through Jesus Christ—to the glory and praise of God. (Phil. 1:3–4, 9–11)

As we think about the members in our home group from church, we can pray for love to spill over from their lives as they know God better. We can pray that they may have deep insight into God's will so they can discern what is best. We can ask God for their purity so that they'll live blamelessly as they await Christ's return. And we can ask God that they be filled with the fruits of upright living and that their lives would bring glory and praise to God.

> We always thank God, the Father of our Lord Jesus Christ, when we pray for you. . . . For this reason, since the day we heard about you, we have not stopped praying for you and asking God to fill you with the knowledge of his will through all spiritual wisdom and understanding. And we pray this in order that you may live a life worthy of the Lord and may please him in every way: bearing fruit in every good work, growing in the knowledge of God, being strengthened with all power according to his glorious might so that you may have great endurance and patience, and joyfully giving thanks to the Father, who has qualified you to share in the inheritance of the saints in the kingdom of light. (Col. 1:3, 9–12)

We might apply these words to our church leaders, asking God to fill them with the knowledge of his will through spiritual wisdom and understanding. We can ask that our children will live a life worthy of God, pleasing him in every way, bearing the fruit of good works. We could pray that husbands will grow in their knowledge of God or that wives will be strengthened with all power, according to God's glorious might, so they can have great endurance and patience. And we can cover all our prayers with joyful thanksgiving because God has qualified us, by Christ's death, to be citizens of the kingdom of light.

> And pray for us, too, that God may open a door for our message, so that we may proclaim the mystery of Christ, for which I am in chains. Pray that I may proclaim it clearly, as I should. (Col. 4:3–4)

As we remember mission teams whom our church has sent out, we can pray that God will open the way for their message of Christ. We can pray that they might speak God's Word faithfully and clearly.

> We always thank God for all of you, mentioning you in our prayers. We continually remember before our God and Father your work produced by faith, your labor prompted by love, and your endurance inspired by hope in our Lord Jesus Christ. (1 Thess. 1:2–3)

As we pray these words of thanks, we can be thankful for the lives of the ones we're praying for, that their faith has produced good works, that their love has prompted labor for the Lord, and that their hope has inspired endurance. After we thank God for these things, we can pray that their faith, love, and hope will continue to produce good works, godly labor, and endurance until Christ's return.

> Now may our God and Father himself and our Lord Jesus clear the way for us to come to you. May the Lord make your love increase and overflow for each other and for everyone else, just as ours does for you. May he strengthen your hearts so that you will be blameless and holy in the presence of our God and Father when our Lord Jesus comes with all his holy ones. (1 Thess. 3:11–13)

We can ask God to give us a chance to fellowship with the ones we're praying for, at the same time asking that their love will increase and overflow. We can ask God to help our love overflow to others. As we pray for Christ to return soon, we can ask the Lord to strengthen our hearts so we will be waiting blameless and holy.

> May God himself, the God of peace, sanctify you through and through. May your whole spirit, soul and body be kept blameless at the coming of our Lord Jesus Christ. The one who calls you is faithful and he will do it. (1 Thess. 5:23–24)

Christ is returning. We can pray that God will set us apart completely and keep our soul and body blameless until the coming of the Lord. We can call on God's faithful promise to do this work in our lives. Then we can extend this prayer to others.

> We ought always to thank God for you, brothers, and rightly so, because your faith is growing more and more, and the love every one of you has for each other is increasing. (2 Thess. 1:3)

We can thank God that the faith of our friends is growing and their love is increasing. Then we can pray that their faith will grow even more and that their love for others will keep on increasing.

> With this in mind, we constantly pray for you, that our God may count you worthy of his calling, and that by his power he may fulfill every good purpose of yours and every act prompted by your faith. We pray this so that the name of our Lord Jesus may be glorified in you, and you in him, according to the grace of our God and the Lord Jesus Christ. (2 Thess. 1:11–12)

We can pray that God will count our friends worthy of his calling. We can ask that every time a certain person's faith in God prompts that person to do something good, God's power will fulfill that person's good intentions. Our prayer should be that the name of the Lord Jesus will be glorified by the way this person lives and acts.

> May our Lord Jesus Christ himself and God our Father, who loved us and by his grace gave us eternal encourage-ment and good hope, encourage your hearts and strengthen you in every good deed and word. (2 Thess. 2:16–17)

We can ask God to encourage the hearts of people we know, strengthening them to speak and do what God wants.

> Finally, brothers, pray for us that the message of the Lord may spread rapidly and be honored, just as it was with you. And pray that we may be delivered from wicked and evil men, for not everyone has faith. (2 Thess. 3:1–2)

We always should pray that the Lord's message will spread rapidly and be honored—especially in areas where people know little or nothing about him. We need to battle in prayer for the ones bringing God's Word to these new areas, asking God to deliver Christian workers from wicked and evil men.

> May the Lord direct your hearts into God's love and Christ's perseverance. (2 Thess. 3:5)

We all need prayer for God's love and perseverance. You might know someone, perhaps a son or daughter, who is wandering from faith. We can pray that God will direct our loved one's heart back into God's love and the endurance of Christ on the cross.

> Now may the Lord of peace himself give you peace at all times and in every way. The Lord be with all of you. (2 Thess. 3:16)

We can request God's peace for members of our Bible study group—peace at all times and in every way. And we can ask the Lord to be with all of them.

> I thank God, whom I serve, as my forefathers did, with a clear conscience, as night and day I constantly remember you in my prayers. (2 Tim. 1:3)

Paul gives thanks as he remembers his disciple Timothy. As we think about that one we've been discipling, we can give thanks and constantly remember him or her in our prayers.

> I always thank my God as I remember you in my prayers, because I hear about your faith in the Lord Jesus and your love for all the saints. I pray that you may be active in sharing your faith, so that you will have a full understanding of every good thing we have in Christ. (Philem. 4–6)

Paul always thanks God as he remembers his friend Philemon. We can give thanks for our friend in the faith who is showing love and hospitality. We can pray that our friend may be active in sharing faith, asking that he or she will have a full understanding of all the good things we have in Christ.

Paul's prayers aimed at the heart of matters. He prayed about things like being filled with love and faith and being strengthened to do good works, and he filled his prayers with thanksgiving. We can use our prayer day to get acquainted with Paul's prayers and use them to direct our requests. As we pray through these prayers, we'll find we're memorizing them. Then we can carry them into our daily prayer lives. When we learn to follow Paul's example of prayer, our prayer lives will never be the same.

eleven

MEMORIZING FOR MEDITATION

I have hidden your word in my heart that I might not sin against you.

—Psalm 119:11

I RECENTLY WOKE UP EARLY IN the morning with a real burden to pray for some friends. Not wanting to wake up my wife, I stayed in bed and prayed. I had been memorizing the book of Philippians, and Paul's prayer in chapter 1 came into my mind, so I began to pray this verse for my friends.

Lord, I pray that their love would abound more and more in knowledge and depth of insight so that they might be able to discern what is best. I pray that you will keep them holy and blameless until your return. And fill them, Lord, with the fruit of righteousness that comes from Jesus Christ. May their lives bring glory and praise to you, Father.

Having Bible verses in my memory bank comes in handy when I'm praying in the dark or driving a car. God often prompts me to use these verses when I pray.

Taking an evening or even a full day for a prayer retreat can seem daunting. What will we do to fill the time when we get tired of praying and reading? A prayer day is a great time for memorizing God's Word. If we're already in the habit of memorizing, we can take the extended time to review and meditate on the Scriptures we have hidden in our hearts. If we've never taken time to memorize Bible verses, we can use a prayer retreat to get started.

I began memorizing Scripture for Sunday school when I was in grade school. Our Sunday school had a Bible memory program with all kinds of trophies and ribbons. I crammed verses into my head early on Sunday mornings, then retained them until I'd said them to the teacher and gotten the trophy for my ribbon. Over the years, I learned enough verses to win a Bible. But I rarely went over the verses again. I hadn't learned the discipline of meditating on the verses I'd memorized. I didn't do too much more memorizing until Bible college when one of our professors, Dr. Garry Friesen, taught us how to use a recipe card box to memorize Scripture.

Recipe Card Box Bible Memory System

This is a simple, no stress way to memorize Bible verses. First, I purchased a recipe or file card box and some three-by-five cards and dividers. Then I created three divisions in the box using the divider cards marked *Daily, Weekly,* and *Monthly.* After writing out two or three verses I wanted to memorize on blank cards, I put them in the section marked *Daily.* Then every day I would read those verses over one time only.

I liked this system because I didn't have to cram the verses into my head the way I did as a child. I just had to read them once daily and put the box away. After about a week, I was surprised to find I'd memorized the verses. When I found I could remember a verse without reading it daily, I put that card in the *Weekly* section. Then I added two or three new verses to my *Daily* section. I would read these new verses once a day. And once a week I read the verses I'd already memorized and shifted to the *Weekly* section. As time went by, I found the weekly verses had become so firm in my mind that I could put them into the *Monthly* section, where I only had to breeze through them once a month.

And the system keeps flowing. As I found new verses I wanted to memorize, I wrote out new cards and put those verses into the *Daily* section. The other verses I had memorized by daily reading were upgraded into the *Weekly* section. At the same time, I graduated some of the weekly verses to the *Monthly* section. Eventually I retired some of the monthly verses and took them out of the box to make room for new verses.

The recipe box method is a less formidable way to start memorizing Scripture. It's great when we see our kids learning verses, but many of us believe we're too old to memorize. Our minds will surprise us. We are capable of memorizing much more than we ever thought possible. The recipe box memory system really works, even for those of us who think we'll never be able to memorize Scripture. We don't even have to think of it as memorizing. We just read the verses once a day for a week or more, and we'll find we have memorized them.

Everyone will make adjustments to the recipe box system to meet their own needs. We each have a different amount of mental retention space and time in our schedules to commit to memorizing Scripture. So, when we fill up our personal memory space, maybe with three or four verses in each section of the file box, we can take out some of the monthly verses to insert new daily verses.

It's good to have new verses flowing into the memory box. At the same time, we'll be amazed at how God will bring those retired verses back into our minds even years later just at the moment we need them for prayer, for encouragement, or as a promise at a difficult time. Once we start memorizing, we can meditate on those verses, use them as we pray, and pull them out to help us stand against temptations of the Evil One. A prayer day is an excellent place to start memorizing.

Memorizing Large Chunks of Scripture

Although I had memorized a great number of verses using the recipe box method, I didn't keep memorizing after Bible college. My recipe box full of verses gathered dust in my office. Then, at a special Sunday school program where my children were getting awards for Bible memory, the teacher had invited an older man to demonstrate his ability to recite Scripture. This man told us how he'd been challenged in his later years to start memorizing whole books of the Bible. Then he quoted the whole book of Philippians for us. I was amazed.

I had thought my brain had become too fossilized to memorize more than a few verses, but this older man had whole books of the Bible in his memory. That encouraged me to try to memorize a whole book. I started by memorizing the book of Titus. I've gone on to memorize Colossians, 1 and 2 Corinthians, the Sermon on the Mount, and 1 and 2 Thessalonians. Because of time limits, with longer books like 1 and 2 Corinthians, I normally retain only three to four chapters at a time. Then as I add a new chapter I drop off an earlier one in much the same way that I would retire verses from my recipe box. When I start memorizing chapter 4, for example, I'll stop reviewing chapter 1 so that my open memory file includes chapters 2–4. And so on.

When I memorize large chunks of Scripture, I still follow the principle of the recipe box. I've internalized the method and read the verses from my Bible instead of writing them on cards. I start by memorizing a paragraph or section, anywhere from two to five verses. In the morning of the first day I'll read it over five, ten, or twenty times, until I can repeat it with my eyes closed. Sometimes I can do this in one session of ten to fifteen minutes. Other times it takes longer.

Then, during that first day, I try to repeat the paragraph several times to cement it. Sometimes I can remember the verses. Often on that first day, I draw a blank. That's okay. That evening I review the verses with a quick read before bedtime. Then I close my eyes and try to repeat the verses. If I get lost, I peek and read the part I'm messing up on. A review before sleeping helps anchor the verses into my subconscious memory, and the next morning, I read the verses again. Once that new paragraph is in my mind, I'll repeat it several times a day.

The section or paragraph I'm learning is like my daily section of the recipe file. I try to review those verses several times daily until I have them memorized. This may take a week or so.

When I have those verses well memorized, I'll push them into a review section called my *Several Times a Week* section. The verses join any previous paragraphs in that chapter that I've already memorized. Those earlier verses are like the weekly section in the recipe file system. I just review them more often, reciting those verses several times each week. I've reviewed these verses in bed, in the car, while jogging, and even while I've been lying on a chiropractor's table.

With those verses in review mode, I'll go back to step one and take another intense reading time to add a new paragraph, or half a paragraph, which I will then read and review several times daily. As the new paragraph becomes familiar, I'll often close my eyes to review my "several times a week" verses and see if I can tack on the new paragraph. After a week or two, depending on how busy my schedule is or the difficulty of the new verses, I usually find that the new paragraph has blended seamlessly in with the earlier sections. Then I'm ready to add new verses.

At least once a week I take time to go over the previous two or three chapters I've memorized. If I've forgotten a phrase or mixed up the order of some words, I do a quick read and correct any mistakes. I compare the periodic reviewing of earlier chapters to the monthly review section in the recipe file method. But because of the volume of verses, I need to review them weekly, not monthly.

Memorizing whole chapters may seem impossible, but I've been amazed at how much quicker I can memorize a group of verses in context than several stand-alone verses. Verses learned in clumps that belong together often tie in with other verses around them and give us clues to help us remember the next bit.

Memorizing Scripture in blocks also helps us understand that book of the Bible. We go over the verses so many times that they become a part of us. We can then take time to meditate on the verses, think about how the book flows, and see how the author repeats certain themes. I knew that one of the themes from 1 Thessalonians was the second coming of Christ. But as I memorized the book and had all five chapters in my memory at the same time, I could see the whole thread of Christ's return weaving its way through the book.

A prayer retreat can be a special time for memorizing God's Word. Start with the recipe box method and then add longer sections later. When we start memorizing, we'll be amazed by how much we can learn and remember. The brain readily responds to a mental workout. The more of God's Word we have in our hearts, the better prepared we will be to live a life that pleases God.

Paul said that God's Word is the "sword of the Spirit" (Eph. 6:17b). The Word is our offensive weapon as we go into battle against the

Evil One. With an array of Bible verses imprinted in our minds, we can pull out the sword when we need it during times of spiritual warfare.

Bible memory isn't just for kids. It can add to our understanding and enjoyment of the Word as we meditate on the Scriptures we have committed to memory. During a prayer retreat we can meditate on verses that are stored in our memory banks, doing so while walking through the woods, playing the verses over in our minds, tasting them with our spirit, and examining them from different angles. Taking time to memorize on a prayer retreat is only the beginning. We'll carry those verses with us. And we'll have started the life-changing discipline of hiding God's Word in our hearts.

twelve

PRAYING WHILE WALKING, KNEELING, DRIVING . . .

When he had said this, he knelt down with all of them and prayed.

—Acts 20:36

WE RECENTLY EXPERIENCED A problem in our ministry. I shared some of the needs with a good friend of mine, and he invited me to pray with him at his house. When I arrived, he handed me a swimsuit and said we'd pray in the hot tub. As we sat in the hot water, pouring our hearts out before the Lord, I had to laugh. Who would have thought of praying in a hot tub? My worries and concerns dissipated as we prayed and the warmth of the water seeped into my tired body. God soothed my heart as the water relaxed my muscles.

We can pray anywhere and in any position. As we plan for a prayer retreat, we need to consider various locations for prayer, different postures, and even different ways of praying. Periodically changing positions or locations is a good way to keep our prayer day moving.

Praying While Kneeling

Scripture speaks of kneeling in prayer (1 Kings 8:54; Ps. 95:6; Eph. 3:14). In the ancient cultures, one kneeled or fell prostrate with one's face to the ground in the presence of a king or great person to show homage (e.g., Gen. 19:1; 48:12; Ruth 2:10; 1 Sam. 25:23, 41). Elijah knelt before God with his face between his knees (1 Kings 18:42). Jesus knelt in the garden before Judas betrayed him (Luke 22:41), but Matthew 26:39 shows that this meant he prostrated himself before the Father. When I was in about fifth grade I was taken on a holiday at Mombasa with my friend Jim Barnett and his family. Dr. Bill Barnett led us in evening devotions, and when it came time to pray, everyone got off their chairs and knelt down. Our family usually prayed in chairs or seated around the table. This was the first time I remember kneeling in prayer.

I don't always kneel when I pray. But especially on prayer days, I usually spend a portion of time on my knees. Sometimes I cheat and use a pillow or sheepskin rug under my knees. When I kneel to pray, I lean over my bed or I put my upper body over a chair. The way we kneel doesn't really matter. But something about kneeling accents my humble position before God and reminds me of my dependence upon him.

Praying While Walking

I enjoy praying while I walk. Some mornings, I'll limit myself to praising God when I am walking and enjoying the stillness and beauty of God's creation. My wife often walks and prays. Some years ago she walked around a one-mile circuit on our mission station in Kenya. During the first mile, she would praise God. During the second mile, she would pray for our family needs and any other requests.

Targeting areas to walk around and pray for, much as the nation of Israel marched around Jericho (Josh. 6:1–16), is another good way to pray. We've participated in city prayer walks, walks around our neighborhood, walks around our mission stations, and prayer walks around abortion clinics. As we walk around a specific area praying for specific needs, the walking makes the prayers more real.

If, on our prayer day, we feel a real burden for one of our children, we can walk around her school as we pray. We can pray protection for our child and pray against the forces of the Evil One that are threatening the life of that school. Or we can walk around inside our child's room, praying that God will bind any works of Satan in the life of our child and claiming that room as a haven for our child. If we have a burden for our church, we can walk and pray around the church building. Or we can do a prayer walk through our neighborhood.

Walking seems to open up our minds and thoughts as we exercise. If it's possible, we should look for a place where we can walk during part of our prayer retreats.

Praying While Lying Down

I do a lot of my praying lying down since I pray in bed late at night or early in the morning. Unfortunately, I often fall asleep while I'm praying. So, on a prayer day, I try not to spend too much prayer time lying down. If I feel tired, I stand up and walk and talk with the Lord as I get my blood circulating. But praying while we're facedown before the Lord is mentioned in the Bible as a position of humiliation and worship. Ezekiel fell facedown and cried out to the Lord when he saw visions and beheld God's glory (Ezek. 1:28; 3:23; 9:8; 43:3; 44:4). Lying flat on our faces before God is symbolic of our humbling ourselves before the God of the universe and is a valid way to spend part of our day in prayer.

Praying While Working

My wife has perfected the art of praying while doing housework. Any task that is fairly mindless can be redeemed and put to good use by praying—as we vacuum, as we fold clothes, or as we sweep. I've found that I can pray while mowing the law. I certainly don't get interrupted, and the roar of the lawn mower engine drowns out the roar of the world.

One reason to have a prayer day is to have a break away from our routine, but on some days we may feel God's urging to dedicate that day to him as a prayer day. Or we may feel a deep burden to pray, yet the everyday business of life will not go away. On those days we can try fasting as a way of reminding our bodies that today is a prayer day. Then as best we can, we can pray as we work. We can have quite an effective day of prayer. And we'll find that as we develop the habit of praying while working, we pray much more, even when we're not having a prayer day.

Praying While Driving

I had to make a long trip some time ago. I decided to make that day a prayer day, focusing on the needs of some of our churches and praying especially for some church leaders. I had almost four hours of uninterrupted prayer time. I quoted Scripture prayers for the church leaders, I sang some praise songs, I pondered some issues and asked God to lead and guide. I had a good time of prayer while driving down the interstate.

I confess that several times I just wanted to reach over, turn on the radio, and just listen to some music. I stopped praying and listened to the radio as I drove through Portland because the traffic jammed up and I had a hard time concentrating on prayer while I dodged other cars.

On another day, I had to preach in a church about three hours away. Pat, a good friend, joined me for the day so we could have a prayer day together. We shared Scriptures and prayed back and forth for most of the trip.

Finding time for a prayer day is often difficult. But we find dead time when we have to drive somewhere. Learn to pray while driving and turn those trips into prayer days.

Or if we love to drive and can't find a quiet place to pray in our homes, we should consider a drive up the mountain or down to the lake or to the coast. We can pray as we drive, walk along the beach, or drive home. A car is a great place to meet with the Lord.

Praying While Sitting

Much of my praying during an at-home prayer day is done while sitting in a comfortable chair. I have my Bible, a comfortable chair, and a notebook. I sit back and read. I close my eyes and pray. But I've been known to sleep in a chair if it's too cozy, so I need to change my position from time to time. I get up and walk. I slide off the chair and kneel with my forehead on the seat of the chair.

Praying While Running

I do a lot of praying on early morning runs. It gets me up and moving and away from the temptation of my pillow. As I run, I praise the Lord. Sometimes thinking about needs and focusing on prayer requests is too difficult as my head gets joggled back and forth. But I'm always able to praise the Lord.

This past year I developed a three-lap circuit around a tree nursery. On the first lap, I praise the Lord. On the second lap, I pray for my family. On the third lap, I recite whatever portion of Scripture I am memorizing at the time.

Although I usually don't run on a prayer day, I did recently. I had received disturbing news and I set aside a day to pray. I started the day pouring my cares and concerns out to God on my early morning run. It gave me focus for the rest of the day of prayer.

Praying While Standing

A common posture of prayer in Israel was to stand. Jesus spoke about the hypocrites who would stand on the street corner and pray so everyone would admire their eloquent prayers (Matt. 6:5). Jesus told a parable in Luke 18:9–14 where the Pharisee stood up to pray. But Jesus said the Pharisee didn't pray to God. He prayed about himself, and God wasn't impressed.

A tax collector had come to pray, and he also stood while he prayed. But he stood at a distance. He wouldn't even look up to heaven. He beat his breast and asked God to have mercy on him. Both men stood as they prayed, but their attitude affected how God heard their prayers.

We can spend part of our prayer day standing in prayer. We're free to raise our hands as a sign of submission to God or to beat our chests in sorrow. The important thing is not whether we stand or sit or kneel as we pray. What counts is coming before God with a humble attitude.

Praying in a Tree House

An early missionary to the Maasai, John Stauffacher knew the importance of setting aside times during his day and days during his week to pray. But he constantly had interruptions at the door—people who needed his help and people who just wanted to visit. Stauffacher finally built a tree house near his home. When he retreated to his tree house and pulled the ladder up, it signaled to everyone that he was praying. They couldn't interrupt him. So he had a chance to be alone with the Lord. I don't know how big the tree house was, so I don't know if he sat or knelt or stood as he prayed. But he created a place where he could pray and meet with God.

All these various postures of prayer can be used as part of a prayer retreat. Breaking up the day by praying in a variety of positions is helpful in keeping concentration or in shifting focus from praise to thanks to requests to listening. We'll also find we can take these different ways of praying and use them in our daily prayer time as well. It really doesn't matter whether we're sitting, walking, running, or kneeling. What's important is finding a place where we can be together with God to pray. Each of us needs our own tree house.

thirteen

FASTING WHILE PRAYING

So after they had fasted and prayed, they placed their hands
on them and sent them off.

—Acts 13:3

WE FAST TO CREATE HUNGER—not just physical hunger, but a hunger
to know God better. Fasting or refraining from food for a period of
time can turn a day of prayer into a deeper, richer spiritual experience. Fasting can also be used to turn a normal workday into a day
of prayer.

Fasting and prayer are often linked. Nehemiah fasted and prayed
when he heard that the walls of Jerusalem were broken down.
David fasted and prayed for the healing of his first son by
Bathsheba. Though Jesus and his disciples were accused of not
fasting like John's disciples and the Pharisees, Jesus did say that
after he left, his disciples would fast (Matt. 9:14–15). And he gave
instructions on fasting in the Sermon on the Mount, when he told
his disciples to fast discreetly without drawing attention to their
fast (Matt. 6:16–18).

The Purpose of Fasting

Fasting is not a formula to get something from God. Fasting doesn't bend God's arm to make him answer us because we deprived ourselves and spent time fasting. The purpose of fasting is to say no to our physical desires and needs for a period of time and focus on God.

Our focus is so much on the physical that we often lose touch with the reality of God and the spiritual realm. Fasting should put us more in tune with the spiritual; then as we pray and listen, we should be more able to discern God's will. When we fast, we tell God that we are more interested in him and in spiritual things than in physical things.

As we taste the sweetness of a closer relationship with God, we should be less drawn to physical pleasures. In Exodus 34, Moses saw God's glory on the mountain and spoke to the Lord for forty days and forty nights without eating or drinking water. God filled him to the point that he seems not to have had a need for physical food. Moses desired God so much that he lost his hunger for food. We too should be happy to give up food or other pleasures to spend time with God.

But I have to be honest. Although I desire to know God better as I grow in my faith, I'm the first to admit that my hunger for God has not quenched my hunger for physical pleasures. I don't willingly give up food for the delight of spending time with God. Maybe I'll get to that stage sometime, but I'm not there yet. For me the physical world is often all-important. I'm tied up with what I eat, what I watch, who I spend time with, and where the rugby game is next weekend. My physical senses are so intensely felt that I often lose touch with God and the spiritual side of things.

Many of us are the same way. Fasting at its beginning stages is usually not what Moses experienced on the mountain where he was so full of God that his physical need for food and water waned. Instead, when we fast, we are telling God we need to starve our physical appetites to reawaken our spiritual hunger for God. We have to wean ourselves off things that distract to reattach our souls with the soul-feeder, God himself.

Fasting from Food

Food can be seen as a symbol for all our physical desires. The most common fast is when we refrain from eating food for a period of time. Before starting his teaching ministry, Jesus went on a forty day fast, during which Satan tempted him. Jesus didn't take any food for that period of time (Matt. 4:1–11; Luke 4:1–13). Far more than Moses, Jesus had a capacity to be filled with his relationship with God the Father. That doesn't mean Jesus in his physical human nature didn't feel physical hunger. Satan tempted Jesus by telling him to turn rocks into bread. His physical hunger must have been intense, but his desire to please God surpassed his hunger.

We can follow Jesus' example and fast for a specified period so we can pray. Often people fast from food, but continue to take fluids, usually water. This is often called a water fast. A water fast allows the body to feel hunger, but the water provides the body with needed fluid. People with health problems should consult their doctors before conducting a complete fast or a water fast.

My friend, Mwaura Njoroge, practiced a once-a-week complete fast. He set aside each Thursday as his day of prayer and fasting. He worked as usual, coming to tea time for prayer with the rest of our staff, but quietly refusing any food or water during that day. He dedicated his normal eating times to prayer.

At other times people will fast from a certain type of food that may be symbolic of pleasure. A common choice is to refrain from desserts as a type of fast. When time for sweet food comes, it is a reminder that our real pleasure is not in fudge brownies or ice cream. No, our pleasure is in the Lord.

Fasting from Other Pleasures

Many of our physical desires are not for outright sinful things. We enjoy sports, hobbies, books, TV, and relationships. None of these things are wrong, but they can distract us from our relationship with God. We can fast from more than just food. We can fast from TV, from reading certain books, from secular music, from playing golf, from fishing, or from any pleasurable activity that keeps us from fully focusing on God.

In 1 Corinthians 7:5, Paul specifically talks about fasting from sexual relations. He writes, "Do not deprive each other except by mutual consent and for a time, so that you may devote yourselves to prayer. Then come together again so that Satan will not tempt you because of your lack of self-control."

Paul says a couple can agree together to refrain from sex for a certain amount of time in order to focus on prayer. But he sets some guidelines: both man and wife should agree, then they should set a specific period of time. And then during that time of sexual fasting, they should devote themselves to prayer.

John Piper in his excellent book on fasting called *A Hunger for God* talks about fasting from sleep. When we get up early to devote time to prayer, when we normally would be sleeping, we are giving up a legitimate pleasure. We are in a sense fasting from sleep and turning that time over to God for prayer.

We can fast in various ways. But the important thing is to use that time of deprivation to turn our physical hunger into a spiritual hunger for God so we can know him better as we devote time to him in prayer. We don't fast from these things to earn God's favor or to feel that God owes us one. The purpose of fasting from such pleasures is to fix our eyes upon God, to be in tune with our spiritual nature and not controlled by our physical appetites.

A Pastor Who Fasts

When Pastor Dave Zetterberg from Lakewood, Washington, takes time to fast, he normally does a water fast, meaning he takes no food, but drinks water only for the period of the fast. He goes about his day as usual and the time he would normally eat he reserves for focused prayer. Other times he takes a full day of fasting and prayer. Instead of gratifying his flesh with food, he prays. Sometimes he does thirty-six-hour fasts and sometimes forty-eight-hour fasts. And while in college, he did a few seventy-two-hour fasts when the school would have weekends of prayer.

Dave feels that fasting helps him to commit the time to come before God. He doesn't feel he's denying himself. As he feels hunger pangs, he's reminded to set his mind on the Lord. After fasting, he feels cleansed in body, mind, and emotions. Dave also fasts occasionally from other things such as TV or music, turning down life's noise and distractions and focusing on the Lord.

Fasting for a College Campus

My son Heath is part of an InterVarsity group at Lewis University. This group set goals for creating spiritual awareness on the campus. They wanted everyone on campus to know about InterVarsity's ministry and set a goal that every student and faculty and staff member would have some kind of encounter with God during a specific week. This week would culminate with a special InterVarsity meeting.

InterVarsity members began praying for this special week each morning at 8 A.M. for half an hour. They prayed to understand God's heart and will for the campus. They prayed that God would take the campus. As they prayed, Heath heard God speaking to him specifically. "If you're serious about this, you've got to fast. If you want to feel my heart, you have to hunger for what I hunger for." As he heard this voice from God, Heath asked, "How long should I fast." The answer was four days.

Heath decided to obey and set the fast time from Sunday evening to Thursday evening, the night of the InterVarsity meeting. He bought some vitamins and Gatorade, and for the next four days, only drank Gatorade and water and took the vitamins. He went to classes as usual, but had a continual attitude of prayer. To his surprise he didn't feel hunger, because his struggle wasn't about food. He didn't even think about food, instead struggling in prayer. As a result, he felt close to God.

Heath had often fasted before when he felt he needed something, but he had treated fasting as a mechanism for manipulating God. He usually didn't finish those fasts. Now he realized that the fasts he had undertaken were selfish. God taught him that true fasting meant taking his mind off himself and his personal desires to see what God wanted. Now Heath wanted to find God's will and purpose. Heath experienced peace, knowing that God would do his will, and that the whole mission was in God's hands.

Heath prayed two to three hours in the afternoons when he didn't have classes. He learned to dwell in God's presence, praying specifically for God's will and for God to show himself to the college community. Some of the time Heath sat silently, meditating quietly before God. At other times he read Scripture and sometimes prayed aloud. Heath felt God's presence in a special way during those four days of fasting, and he knew he was being strengthened by something other than food.

Heath read a lot from John about obeying God and abiding in the vine. John 14:21 spoke to him strongly: "Whoever has my commands and obeys them, he is the one who loves me. He who loves me will be loved by my Father, and I too will love him and show myself to him." This verse and others made it clear that being in God's presence meant listening to his voice and then obeying. To know God meant obeying what Heath already knew. Then God would reveal more. Heath felt challenged to remain and to abide in the vine.

On Thursday evening Heath ate and felt like he hadn't fasted at all. The evening event at InterVarsity attracted almost sixty people (normally only thirty to forty would attend). More important, the members felt the working of the Spirit. The group experienced a real call back to prayer, with up to twenty coming to daily morning prayers after the event.

After the fast, Heath continued on with the habit of praying two to three hours a day, in the same enhanced state of spiritual awareness. He felt a growing sense of trusting God and committing his life to serve God no matter what the cost.

The next week Heath felt God wanted him to pray for a Muslim girl he had met. Immediately he wanted to fast, but instead he heard God's voice saying he shouldn't fast but should pray the way he had during the fast. So Heath did so. Heath learned that God uses fasting at certain times for certain purposes. We may not always understand what God wants in a time of fasting, but if he calls us to fast, the most important thing is to obey.

A Poison-Maker's Fast

Two years ago I went with Menye Keneiya, a Dorobo hunter in Kenya, to watch him make arrow poison. As I observed him cutting branches from the *olmorijo* tree, peeling the bark, and boiling the sticks in water to make the poison, I listened to the old man's lore. Making arrow poison is a spiritual event to the Dorobo. It had to be done properly and with reverence for God the creator. The poison-maker had to abstain or fast from certain things for four days before making poison. Menye Keneiya told me he had not put any salt on his food, nor had he eaten any fat. He had abstained from sexual relations with his wife, and he had not used soap on his body. According to their tradition, breaking any of these fasts would result in impotent arrow poison.

A Dorobo hunter will fast from those types of things for four days to get good arrow poison. Shouldn't we as Christians show the same discipline as we seek a deeper relationship with God? We should obey God and include fasting as part of our prayer in order to approach God humbly and to starve our physical appetites, especially as we desire to know the Lord better. And what better place to start practicing the spiritual discipline of fasting than on a personal prayer retreat?

fourteen

WRESTLING WHILE WE PRAY

Epaphras . . . is always wrestling in prayer for you, that you may stand firm in all the will of God, mature and fully assured.

—Colossians 4:12

WE OFTEN DON'T REALIZE THAT we are in a battle. We need to adjust our prayers into a heightened state of battlefield readiness. Paul wrote in Ephesians 6:12, "Our struggle is not against flesh and blood but against the rulers, against the authorities, against the powers of this dark world and against the spiritual forces of evil in the heavenly realms." As we see the whole picture of the cosmic struggle between Satan and his minions and God and his kingdom of light, we can arm ourselves and be alert in prayer. Wrestling in prayer, or warfare praying, should be a vital part of any prayer day.

Praying Out Demons

I heard a murmuring in the church and people shifted to make way as a young Kenyan girl wearing only a petticoat pushed her way into a crowded row and started chewing on the wooden pews, disrupting the service. The church leaders escorted her outside and the service continued. Later in the day I saw the girl on the side of the road. Her eyes looked vacant. Did she have a demon? Or was she just crazy?

I knew I should do something, but didn't know where to start. I knew that whatever the source of the girl's problems, we should pray for the girl and help her. Later that afternoon about eight of us missionaries agreed we should try to help this lost girl. Dr. Jay Rupp got the girl admitted to the hospital for a few days and we gathered to pray.

As we circled in the hospital chapel and prayed for the girl, whose name was Rose, it became evident she had a demon. I felt scared, and others also felt nervous. We recruited from the coast a Kenyan Bible school student who had experience in casting out demons. We trusted God and began to pray, making some progress that first Sunday afternoon. But we knew the battle wasn't over. I went home, burdened for Rose, and looked for help in how to pray. I borrowed a couple of books on praying against demons. I knew that in Christ we had the authority to stand against Satan, but I really didn't know how to pray. We met again the next morning at about 6 A.M. to pray for Rose for one hour. We did that throughout the week and added a few late afternoon prayer hours as well.

By the end of the week, we had discerned that the evil spirits had gained control of Rose's mind through her membership in a cult and through a harmful relationship with her father. When she willingly forgave her father for various forms of abuse in her childhood, her forgiveness removed Satan's right to stay. As God removed Satan's strongholds by prayer, he delivered Rose from Satan's power.

We commanded a number of different demons to leave Rose and they did.

Praying with that team for Rose's deliverance opened my eyes to a new level of prayer, often called warfare praying. I had always believed Satan was real, and I had often prayed the Lord's prayer—that the Father would deliver me from him. But this was the first time I'd had to wrestle so openly with the Evil One. I thank God for my partners in prayer as we all cried out to Jesus to help us during that week with Rose.

We Are in a Battle

I began to see that we as Christians are in a pitched battle. We just don't realize it all of the time. Prayer is a struggle against the powers of darkness and the spiritual forces of evil. As we realize the nature of our warfare, we can pray and win the victory because we're prepared and ready.

Warfare praying is not limited to times when someone's life has been totally given over to Satan and they have a demon, as we encountered with Rose. Satan has many crafty ways of ambushing Christians and sidelining them. He builds strongholds in our lives—strongholds of anger, strongholds of lust and impurity, and strongholds of fear—and in the lives of our friends and families. He gains these strongholds or footholds when certain areas in our lives are given over to Satan by our refusal to repent of sin. Once a stronghold starts, Satan works hard at building it into a fortress that we think can never be overthrown—strongholds of addiction and strongholds of drunkenness.

Strongholds can be destroyed with prayer. Paul wrote in 2 Corinthians 10:4, "The weapons we fight with are not the weapons of the world. On the contrary, they have divine power to demolish strongholds."

We need to be able to pray strong warfare prayers as we stand against the Evil One in our times of prayer. As we learn to expand our prayer lives and set aside extended periods of time to pray, we need some warfare prayers in our arsenal.

A Prologue to Warfare Prayer

Over the years, I've learned that before going into battle with Satan over some issue, it's important to remind myself and Satan of the truth. I have a prologue-to-warfare prayer that I pray out loud so Satan can hear it. It goes something like this.

> Satan, I remind you that you are a created being. Jesus Christ created you and he is greater than you. I remind you that Jesus Christ died on the cross and that by his death Jesus disarmed you and triumphed over you. After his resurrection, Jesus Christ was seated in the heavenly realms at the right hand of God the Father, where he is high above all rule and authority, power and dominion, and every title that can be given. All things are under the feet of Jesus. I also remind you, Satan, that as a believer in Jesus whose sins have been cleansed by his blood, I have been raised with Christ and I am now seated with Christ in the heavenly realms. So from that position of authority given to me, not because of who I am, but only because of what Jesus has done for me, I pray against you, Satan, in the powerful name of Jesus.

I then go on to pray about the concerns and strongholds confronting me, often calling on the name of Jesus and the power of his blood as I pray against Satan and his clever schemes.

This prologue to prayer sets the stage and reminds me of what

Christ has done and his position and authority. It also reminds me of who I am in Christ and the power we have as Christians to pray against the dominion and power of Satan in this world.

Each element of this prologue to warfare prayer is based on Scripture. Colossians 1:16 tells us Jesus created everything, including things in heaven and on earth, visible and invisible, thrones or powers or authorities. Satan is clearly included in this creation. All were created by Christ and for Christ, and Colossians 1:18 points out that Christ has the supremacy in everything. Colossians 2:15 shows Christ disarming the powers and authorities and triumphing over them at the cross. Ephesians 1:20–22 speaks of Christ being raised from the dead and seated at God's right hand high above all rule, authority, power, and dominion. And Ephesians 2:6 shows that we as believers have been seated with Christ in the heavenly realms.

Praying on the Armor

Another important step in preparing for warfare prayer is to pray on the full armor of God that is listed in Ephesians 6. I have memorized the spiritual armor that Paul mentions, and as I enter into a wrestling match with the Evil One, I try to remember to put on each piece of the armor. I first put on the belt of truth. As I pray, I remind myself of the truth of who I am and who Satan is. The prologue-to-warfare prayer is the truth. I remind myself of the truth of what Jesus did at the cross. Once I have the truth solidly in my mind, the rest of the armor has a place to hang.

I visually pull on the breastplate of righteousness. I know I'm not righteous, but I know I'm counted righteous because of Christ's death on the cross. I thank God for the fact that he sees me as righteous through the blood of Christ. Then I pray and confess any sinful thoughts or actions and ask for forgiveness so that I stand righteous as I start to pray.

I think about my feet, which have on sandals ready to go out and carry the gospel of peace to a world that's been separated from God.

I take up the shield of faith. I ask God to strengthen my faith in him so that when the arrows of the Evil One come, they will be absorbed by the shield. I remind myself of God's power and promises as a way to increase my faith. And I ask that, when Satan hurls discouraging things at me, God would help me to overcome them through faith.

I put on my helmet, which is salvation. I remind myself that I have been saved by Christ's work on the cross. And I pray that if Satan attacks my mind to make me think I'm worthless or not really saved, then I can fall back on the truth that surrounds my mind like a helmet. I am saved. God loves me and he saved me.

Finally, I pick up my sword, the Word of God. When Satan tempted Eve, he questioned the Word of God. "Did God really say, 'You must not eat from any tree in the garden?'" (Gen. 3:1). His tactics against Jesus in the wilderness also involved twisting God's Word (Matt. 4:1–11; Luke 4:1–13). I know I need God's Word to fight against Satan. I need to know what it says in order to counterattack when Satan brings doubts about God's Word. I pray that God will bring to my mind verses and passages I've memorized as I pray.

After Paul tells us to put on the full armor of God, his final command in Ephesians 6:18 is to pray: "And pray in the Spirit on all occasions with all kinds of prayers and requests. With this in mind, be alert and always keep on praying for all the saints." That verse is full of the word *all*. Pray on *all* occasions. Pray with *all* kinds of prayers. Pray with *all* kinds of requests. *Always* keep on praying. Pray for *all* the saints.

Praying Against the Evil One

Once we have reminded Satan of the truth and put on the armor of God, we can then follow Paul's command to pray and focus our prayers against the power of Satan. As we pray, we need to target the enemy, and if there's a particular stronghold, we need to speak verbally against it.

I remember some years ago praying against a spirit of greed that had crept into our church. As I prayed, I confronted Satan and this spirit and commanded the spirit of greed to release its grip on the church. In a similar fashion, my wife and I have been involved in praying against a spirit of anger and have pinpointed our prayers against that spirit and commanded it to leave. In a more general sense, I have wrestled in prayer against a spirit of drunkenness that holds many Dorobo men and women captive. In praying about abortion-on-demand, I have prayed against a spirit of selfishness.

In each prayer, we start with the truth of who God is, then zero in on the particular area where Satan has built a stronghold, and then command him to leave, using the authority of Scripture, Jesus' name, and his blood. As we pray, we also need to ask for protection for ourselves and those around us, for Satan will often try to lash out. This kind of praying should not be undertaken lightly. If we're praying warfare prayers, there will most likely be a reaction from the Evil One. He will try to confuse us, accusing us of sins in our past. That's why, as we pull on the breastplate of righteousness, it's so important to have confessed our sins and covered them with Christ's blood.

As Satan counterattacks, we can claim the victory in the name of Jesus, calling on the blood of Christ to protect us. While we prayed for Rose, we met strong resistance when she needed to forgive her father. She refused and, because of her refusal to forgive, continued to harbor the spirits that troubled her.

One of our group started singing, "There is power, power, wonder-working power in the blood of the Lamb." We sang those words over and over until suddenly Rose said she wanted to forgive her father. The demons submitted to the shed blood of Christ, because there is power in the blood of Christ. Using phrases like "in the name of Jesus" and "by the blood of Jesus" aren't magical chants. They are a repetition in prayer of truth from God's Word that galls Satan and drives him away.

Another good way to put Satan on his back foot is to praise the Lord. It seems Satan can't abide where God's praises are ringing out. We've often started a session of warfare praying with a time of praise.

We are in a battle. Satan is the enemy. We need to be armed and ready for battle, and we need to enter into the fray by prayer. There are all kinds of prayers and requests, but as we learn to stand against the Evil One, it is certainly important to have warfare prayer in our arsenal.

We've only brushed the surface of warfare praying. Since this is such a demanding type of praying, I recommend the following reading list for more in-depth understanding of this type of prayer.

Anderson, Neil T. *The Bondage Breaker.* Eugene, Ore.: Harvest House, 1990.

———. *Victory over the Darkness: Realizing the Power of Your Identity in Christ.* Ventura, Calif.: Regal Books, 1990.

Anderson, Neil T. and Timothy M. Warner. *The Beginner's Guide to Spiritual Warfare.* Ann Arbor, Mich.: Servant Publications, 2000.

Bubeck, Mark I. *The Adversary: The Christian Versus Demon Activity.* Chicago: Moody, 1975.

———. *Overcoming the Adversary.* Chicago: Moody, 1984.

———. *Spiritual Warfare Prayers.* Chicago: Moody, 1997.

———. *Preparing for Battle.* Chicago: Moody, 1999.

Kraft, Charles H. *Christianity with Power: Your Worldview and Your Experience of the Supernatural.* Ann Arbor, Mich.: Vine Books, 1989.

————. *Defeating Dark Angels: Breaking Demonic Oppression in the Believer's Life.* Ann Arbor, Mich.: Vine Books, 1992.

fifteen

WATCHING GOD WORK AS WE PRAY

So Peter was kept in prison, but the church was earnestly praying to God for him. . . . He went to the house of Mary the mother of John, also called Mark, where many people had gathered and were praying. . . . But Peter kept on knocking, and when they opened the door and saw him, they were astonished.

—Acts 12:5, 12, 16

WHEN GOD DOES ANSWER THE prayers of his people we are astonished. As we set aside time to pray and meet with God, we will see amazing and even unbelievable answers.

An Angel Springs Peter

Peter had been thrown into prison. The church gathered at night at Mary's house to keep an earnest prayer vigil for their captive leader. As they prayed, God answered by sending an angel, who woke Peter up and released him from his chains before leading him out through the prison gates. When Peter arrived at the prayer meeting, a servant girl named Rhoda answered the door. She ran back to announce to the others that Peter stood at the door. They didn't believe her, but they told her she'd lost her mind. But Peter kept on knocking. When they opened the door and saw him standing there in answer to their earnest prayers, they were astonished (Acts 12:1–19).

As we take time to pray, God works. It's a mystery why God would choose to answer our prayers, but Jesus told us to ask and we would receive (Matt. 7:7–11). He also taught us to pray according to God's will (Matt. 6:10). James wrote that the prayer of a righteous man is powerful and effective (James 5:16). When the early church prayed Peter out of prison, they couldn't believe it. They had witnessed a miracle. As they had gathered and prayed, they had gotten in tune with the Lord and prayed according to his will. God still had work for Peter to do and God freed him from prison.

As we pray and meet with our God, we will learn to pray for his will. As we understand God's will, it may change our requests. We may discover our desires aren't God's will for that situation. As we watch God answer our needs in a different way than we had planned, we can be confident God is still in control. God does answer our prayers.

God Speaks in the Desert

Pat Thurman worked in Egypt as a missionary with Operation Mobilization (OM). Their OM leader had been blacklisted for his Christian activities and had to leave the country. Pat and some of the other men on the OM team were left to carry on. They wanted to know God's direction for their mission in Egypt, so they drove out of

Cairo to a petrified forest about twenty miles south of the city. They pulled off the road and drove down into a wadi, or small valley. The men sat in the VW van, talking and praying about what they wanted to see happen in Egypt. As they prayed, God gave them a vision of Egyptian Christians who would take their faith to other countries in the Arab world. They began to pray for God to raise up what they called a Gideon's army, a band of three hundred Egyptian Christians who would boldly share Christ with other Arabs.

After that prayer day in the desert, Pat listened to a sermon tape about a missionary who had been arrested by the communists in China. He gave his testimony. The communists had isolated him and then constantly interrogated him as they tried to force him to sign a paper saying he was guilty of crimes against the new government. He became so tired his eyes could barely focus. When one of the interrogators came in and snapped on the light, the missionary saw a phrase written in Chinese characters on the wall above the guard, and he read it out loud. "My times are in your hands; deliver me from my enemies and from those who pursue me."

The guard demanded to know where the missionary had gotten the phrase. The missionary said it came from the Bible. The guard found a Chinese Bible and pushed it in front of the missionary, ordering him to find those words in the Bible. The exhausted missionary could hardly see and he had no idea where to start looking for the verse. But he prayed and opened the Bible. It fell open to the very verse in the Psalms he'd quoted. This amazed the guard so much he later became a Christian.

That story from the tape echoed in Pat's mind when OM later asked him to lead the OM team in Egypt. He felt the burden of such responsibility, and he drove out alone to the same desert wadi to pray and seek God's guidance in this new job. As he sat in the van, praying in the desert, he thought about the story of the missionary from China. Pat wanted to read that verse, but didn't know where to find it, and he prayed, asking God to show him the verse. When he picked up his Bible, it opened right to Psalm 31:15 and he read, "My times are in your hands; deliver me from my enemies and from those who pursue me." Pat took this as a sign and a promise from the Lord that his times were in God's hands and the Lord would protect him in the new responsibilities he faced.

The Lord also confirmed in Pat's heart that he and the OM team in Egypt should take up the vision to pray for three hundred Egyptian Christians to spread out into the Arab world. Pat's team made the discipling of Egyptian believers one of the top priorities of their ministry. Although that prayer has not yet been fully answered, Pat and others continue to pray that God will fulfill that vision.

God Answers Prayer Group

Pastor Samuel Ng'ang'a ministers in churches along Diani Beach in Kenya. He and three other pastors formed a prayer fellowship several years ago after they held a prayer day for a special fund raising project. God answered their prayers from that prayer day and they raised almost $1,000.

The pastors decided to continue to meet for a prayer day once a month. Three years later the group now has twelve pastors. They normally start at 8 A.M. with a time of singing and sharing the Word. Then they pray. Each month they have a different focus for prayer. In November 2000, they held a day of prayer and fasting so they could seek God's face. At other times they listen to speakers or study the Bible together. But they always share prayer items and pray for each other, and they feel their burdens lighten as they leave their needs with the Lord.

One pastor in the group felt God calling him to leave his church and join a nationwide children's ministry. The pastors in the fellowship prayed about this decision. God brought another pastor to lead the church at the same time God opened a door for this pastor to join the children's ministry. Two years later he became its director.

Pastor Ng'ang'a asked the fellowship to pray that he might be able to study further, and God opened a door for him to join a degree program at a Bible school in Kitale, Kenya.

Emotional Crisis

In March 1990, Dave Zetterberg collapsed emotionally. He had been working a full-time job of nine to eleven hours a day in a warehouse, and he held a part-time position in a church. At the church, Dave covered the youth group and the young married couples, led music and worship, did some of the preaching, and sat on the church board. The church had difficult leadership issues. Dave and his wife, Denise, had three kids under the age of four, and with Dave's schedule, he rarely saw Denise. It was tough on their marriage.

One Monday when Dave had to get up at 5 A.M. for work, he slept through his alarm. He woke up at 9 A.M. and rushed to work, arriving several hours late. He walked into his boss's office, sat down, and broke down. Dave felt completely drained emotionally, mentally, and physically. Dave's boss, a Christian, talked and prayed together with Dave. Then he told Dave to take the week off.

Dave and Denise went to the Lord in prayer during that week to ask, "God, what do you want us to do?" They spent the week catching up on rest and on each other. They held a thirty-six-hour fast and prayed during the times they would have eaten. Dave asked God hard questions. "God, I can't keep on doing this." Dave had felt that God expected him to keep on with the insane schedule, and he felt he was "doing it for God."

The couple prayed and were honest with each other and with God. Dave didn't pray the way he felt he was supposed to pray as a

Christian. Instead, he told God that it wasn't fair for God to have put him in such a difficult situation. He asked God why he was putting them through these hard experiences that were harming their marriage?

As Dave prayed, God spoke quietly. Dave realized he'd been doing some things and taking on some responsibilities in his own strength and then trying to make them work for God. God showed Dave that much of what he had taken on wasn't really what God had in mind for him. As Dave prayed, he began to see the spiritual obligation he felt toward the church did not come from God. Dave carried his own sense of obligation and felt he had to hold the church together.

By the end of the week, Dave had sensed from his prayer time that he should resign his position in the church. The Lord confirmed this as Dave and Denise sat and discussed how they'd been praying and what they'd heard from the Lord. They realized God was more interested in them having a healthy marriage than in having them serve the church. God showed Dave his first obligation was to his family, and Dave turned in his resignation at the end of June.

Dave had no immediate plans. God showed Dave that he should resign from that church but didn't give him a timetable of what would come next. Dave and Denise knew that God wanted them in ministry full time, but they felt unsure of what step to take next. Dave hadn't even put together a résumé.

Dave returned to work at the warehouse and within ten days he had a call from Pastor Mark Nordtvedt, who was looking for an associate pastor at the Church at Lakewood in Lakewood, Washington. He asked Dave out for lunch to talk about the position. Dave went to the lunch right from his job at the warehouse, sweaty and dusty and not in a great state of mind for the interview.

Mark had heard about Dave from a friend who had been the music director at Dave's home church. Mark had carried Dave's phone number around for five months before he finally called to set up the appointment. And in God's timing, the call came ten days after Dave's resignation. Mark and Dave met a few more times, and by early September, Mark offered Dave the job of associate pastor. Dave started working at the Church at Lakewood the end of September 1990.

By taking time in a crisis to pray and seek God's direction, God gave Dave and Denise hope for their marriage and brought Dave into a positive church situation where he was able to serve for four years as an associate pastor under a good role model before becoming the senior pastor.

Prayer Vigil Scholarship

Joseph Kim, a missionary to Kenya, often wakes up around 4 A.M. and goes to his prayer room for two hours of prayer. When he's home in Korea, he goes to his church at that time to pray. As he prays, he spends time in praise and worship of the Lord before asking the Lord for guidance in various matters. Then he meditates on a passage from the Bible, finding things to pray about from his Bible reading. He also plans a special week of fasting and prayer each year for his spiritual refreshment.

Joseph and his wife held an all night prayer vigil when he needed a scholarship for further studies at Wheaton Graduate School. Joseph had gone to Korea in 1990 for home assignment, but he wanted to attend Wheaton Graduate School to evaluate his mission work and to be better equipped for missionary service. He applied to Wheaton College and asked for a scholarship, but they told him there was not much hope for a scholarship because of the high number of applicants from countries poorer than Korea.

Joseph and his wife decided to spend the whole night in Korea praying for God to give them the needed scholarship. They held this prayer vigil at the same time the scholarship committee met to make a decision on how to award scholarships. The following morning Joseph received a phone call from Wheaton. "Joseph, congratulations! You have got the scholarship. Prepare to come to Wheaton." The Kims went to Wheaton in August 1990 with a scholarship to cover his expenses for one year as Joseph studied for his master's degree in intercultural studies.

Miracle Baby

John and Sandy Nelson stood in total disbelief. An amniocentesis test indicated an abnormality in their unborn baby. A special gene-mapping test determined the baby had a partially missing eighteenth chromosome in the lower right hand corner, a rare condition doctors call 18 Q syndrome. The news devastated John and Sandy. Stunned, they hardly knew what to do next. Ultrasound examinations revealed major problems—three heart chambers instead of four, cleft palate, deformities in the skull, abnormal spherical brain separation, a twisted abdomen, calcification of the liver, deformed hands, one deformed foot, and more.

John remembers, "We were just crushed." During the first week as they tried to absorb the news, they didn't know whether to pray for a miracle or to hope the baby would not survive the pregnancy. Doctors encouraged the Nelsons to seek a late-term abortion. Sandy was four-and-a-half months pregnant and this was her fourth child.

When the Nelsons talked to their pastor's wife she said, "We need to be praying for a miracle." John remembers being doubtful. He thought the pastor's wife just didn't understand the seriousness of the condition. During that first week, as they shared and received counsel from the pastoral staff and their own family, the Nelsons felt in their hearts the baby would not survive the pregnancy, and then life would go on.

A week later an echocardiogram showed the heart now had four chambers. The Nelsons faced the reality the baby could be born alive. Instead of selfishly praying, "Lord, take this baby," their attitude became, "Lord, that's one problem down. How many more to go?"

The first Sunday after the devastating news, the Nelsons had walked into church and immediately broke down crying. Caring members took them aside and began to pray. They held a healing service for John and Sandy and for the baby. John didn't honestly believe that God would perform a healing for him—he didn't feel he was important enough in God's scheme of things for such a powerful miracle. But the church convinced them that God wanted to use this situation to perform a great miracle. This infused John and Sandy with the courage to pray.

After the test showed the baby now had four heart chambers, the Nelsons launched a national prayer chain by e-mail. They sent e-mails, explaining the problems their baby faced and asking people to pray. They also asked people on their list to pass on the requests to others. Thousands prayed as part of the e-mail prayer chain. John's father's church of fourteen hundred members took time for regular corporate prayer for the baby.

They designated certain days as special times of prayer for particular health problems. The first prayer day focused on the baby's heart. John says they entered into prayer haphazardly and with weak faith. Over four months or so, they had three or four special days dedicated to prayer and fasting. They received dozens of encouraging e-mail responses.

So they kept on praying, putting out requests and watching God answer. Teams of prayer partners got on their knees for specific medical problems. The doctors did ultrasound imaging every week, and they kept seeing improvement in various parts of the baby's body, although the hands still looked like curled claws. John felt a special burden for the hands. He wanted his daughter to have perfect hands so she could praise God with music. But two weeks before the delivery, ultrasounds still showed hand deformity.

They kept praying. Sometimes small groups gathered to pray. Often people prayed on their own. On days designated for fasting, John would take his normal lunch hour for prayer instead of eating.

On April 22, 1999, doctors decided to induce labor. John and Sandy had talked with doctors from the neonatal intensive care unit on what type of resuscitative measures to take. The doctors expected severe trauma for the baby and gathered a team of medical experts for the birth. The delivery went great. As their daughter Rebekah was born, John, heart racing, looked at her hands. They were normal. Rebekah's skull was fine, she had no cleft palate, and her foot was okay. They couldn't tell about internal problems, but they didn't need the respiratory specialist. John says, "Never before have so many doctors been paid so much to do so little."

Complete ultrasounds of Rebekah's body showed no abnormalities. Brain scans came back normal. Doctors decided they must have been mistaken about the chromosomal problem, so they ran another chromosomal screen. The test showed that Rebekah did still have the chromosomal abnormality; it wasn't just a case of poor testing and mistaken diagnosis. God, in his power, healed Rebekah from massive deformities as John and Sandy, their church, and thousands of others took blocks of time out of their days to pray for a miracle.

The chromosomal abnormality still looms like a dark cloud. Rebekah is now twenty-six months and has a condition called hypertomia or lack of muscle tone. She isn't walking yet, but she can stand. Her appetite is severely suppressed and she may suffer from a lack of human growth hormone. Twice Rebekah has had serious medical bouts as dehydration from lack of eating has shut her system down, and she's suffered brain seizures.

Doctors, concerned about Rebekah's slow growth and inability to eat well, scheduled surgery to fit her with a feeding tube in June 2001. The operation went well, and as of this writing Rebekah is learning to tolerate the feeding tube. John and Sandy know there may still be rough spots in the road for their fourth child. And they know they need to keep on praying. But they're thrilled by what they've seen. They realize nothing is impossible with God.

Watch Out for Hippos

As we plan prayer retreats, we will find our relationship with God grows deeper. We will discover his guidance and see his marvelous answers to prayer. But Satan will do whatever he can to distract us from intense, focused times of prayer. A few years ago he used a hippo to derail my prayer time.

We had scheduled a day of prayer and fasting at our monthly discipleship course for new Dorobo Christians. We gathered at our training center by the shores of Lake Naivasha. We spent several hours in worship, praise, and thanksgiving. Then we sent everyone outside to find a quiet spot for an hour alone with God to confess any sins and seek God's face.

I sat under a massive yellow fever tree by the lake's edge. I set my Bible and notebook on the grass nearby, leaned my back against the tree, and began to pray. Soon I heard noises in the bushes behind me, rustling noises. Since Maasai herdsmen often bring their livestock to drink at the lake, I assumed someone had left a cow or a goat rummaging in the bushes. I continued to pray and listen to the Lord. Then I saw a young Maasai man, dressed in a red cloth, carrying a spear as he walked carefully behind the bushes. I tried to ignore the commotion, thinking he would collect his lost goat and go away.

The cracking and breaking of branches became louder, and the

Maasai man shouted out in Swahili, "Kiboko!" meaning "hippo." With my prayers forgotten, I jumped up and saw the bushes part as a bull hippo burst out, running for the water. I hid behind the tree, and the hippo narrowly missed trampling my Bible as he sprinted for the safety of the lake, splashing noisily into the water. Others from our group came running to see what had happened. After we all calmed down, I tried to get back into a contemplative mood for prayer, but the hippo had made a hash of my silent time with God.

Distractions from prayer will be never ending. The best way to overcome distractions is by pulling away, as Jesus did, to a lonely place to pray. We need to plan prayer retreats. They won't happen unless we purposefully schedule them into our lives. Even if we can't schedule a whole day, we need to find blocks of time where we can ignore the distractions of life and meet with God to pray. Jesus got up very early to be alone with the Father. God wants us to spend time with him, and we need to take time to renew our relationship with the Lord. If we want to know God better, we need to make a date with God.

SAMPLE PRAYER DAY SCHEDULE

HERE'S ONE POSSIBLE WAY TO organize a personal prayer day. It's meant only as a rough guide to basic elements in a quality day with the Lord.

This plan is divided into eight one-hour segments, but some may want to spend more time in praise. Others may have a list of needs they want to pray for and will spend more time giving their requests to God. Confession sometimes takes a whole morning. Others may choose not to memorize and can dedicate that time for more praying or listening. We may not have a full day, in which case it is necessary to cut down the time segments.

8 A.M.   *Praise.* Spend a full hour praising God from the Psalms and other praise-filled passages. Listen to praise music.

9 A.M.   *Confession.* Confession is crucial to a right relationship with God, so set aside enough time to examine your heart and allow God to point out any sins to confess. Then ask God for forgiveness.

191

10 A.M.   *Thanksgiving.* Take a walk for an hour in a nearby park while thanking God for his blessings.

11 A.M.   *Pray for family.* Using some of Paul's requests, pray for the needs of family and others.

noon   *Read Scripture.* Choose a passage from the Bible and savor it, reading slowly, praying back to God the truths you've learned.

1 P.M.   *Memorize Scripture.* Memorize a few verses to carry with you for the weeks ahead. Meditate on them during this hour.

2 P.M.   *Listen.* Sit quietly, listen to the Lord. If you need guidance, ask God for wisdom. Then listen. If you just want him to affirm his love for you, God will use verses that you've read and memorized to encourage and comfort you as you listen.

3 P.M.   *All kinds of prayers and requests.* Using Jesus' requests for God to be glorified and for unity among believers, pray for our church leaders, for our nation's political leaders, and for other requests.

We can organize our time with God in many different ways. The most important matter is to set aside the time and follow through.